CONTROL YOUR BUILD

R J Winters

Many "how to build your own home" books are out there. This is not one of those books! Who has the time in his or her very busy life to be a general contractor? This book recommends that you hire a builder to build your new home just keep an eye on him by controlling your build.

WWW.CONTROLYOURBUILD.COM

This book is intended to give general information on new home construction. Although every consideration was taken to ensure all material in book is accurate as possible, the author and publisher assume no responsibility for errors or omissions. The author recommends that the readers do all their homework and seek the advice and guidance of professional and legal agents to assist them with any final decisions.

Copyright © 2013 R J Winters
All rights reserved.
ISBN: 0615817106
ISBN 13: 9780615817101
Library of Congress Control Number: 2013909272
RJ Winters Williamsville, NY

TABLE OF CONTENTS

Table of Contents

CHAPTER 21
Tools to Keep You in Control
103

CHAPTER 22
Final Notes
133

INTRODUCTION

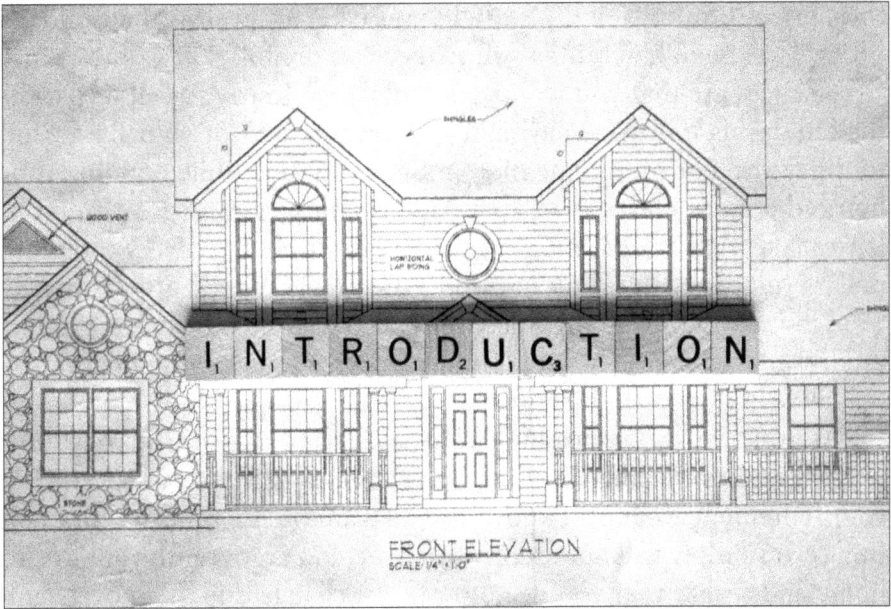

The average person is always short on two things: *time* and *money*! It always seems that when you have the time, you don't have the money, and when you have the money, you never seem to have the time. Reading this book and putting the lessons learned to work will allow anyone to save time and money while building the home of his or her dreams.

Many "how to build your own home" books are out there. This is not one of those books! Who has the time in his or her very busy life to be a general contractor? This book recommends that you hire a builder to build your new home. Don't take valuable time away from what you do best; let the professional builder do the work. This book is intended to help buyers beware and is designed to help future homeowners stimulate their minds by allowing them to control their builds. Lessons presented in this book will help anyone select the right people, from an architect to the best builder. Selecting the right people will mitigate problems, save money, and allow you to build the perfect home. It will also help you keep an eye on the builder's progress as he or she builds your American dream.

Chances are that you will need a mortgage to pay for all or part of the build; this mortgage payment will become part of your life for up to thirty years or more. The more money you save while building your home, the less interest you will pay back. Let me give you a great example. If you take a thirty year mortgage at 5 percent interest, every thousand dollars you save while building your house will save you approximately $932 in interest during the thirty year loan as well as the original thousand you saved on the house. That leaves you a total savings of approximately $1,932.00 over thirty years.

As you can see, controlling your build can save you money both upfront and over time. Wouldn't you rather have an extra $1,932.00 in your retirement account? I know I would. Don't waste time or money on things you simply will not use, or worse yet, don't move into your dream home and realize that you need to make a change due to an oversight. Both will cost you on the front and the back ends. Let's face it: this will most likely be one of the most expensive and important projects you will go through, whether you do it by yourself or with a significant other. The best thing you can do is buy this book, keep it close to you as you design and build your home, and do your homework.

Throughout the book, I will talk continuously about doing your homework. I cannot emphasize enough how important this is. Like anything else in life, there is always homework. Chapters 1 and 2 are the most important chapters in the book. There is a lot of homework here.

Procrastination is the thief of opportunity. Do yourself a huge favor: Read the entire book first and then design a good building plan. This is your opportunity to help yourself get the job done with minimal problems and save thousands of dollars. Good luck. Now, go save some money! We will start out right away with the first task you will need to perform: risk management. You will need to identify all risks involved in building a home. Chapter 1 will help you with this process. Before you sign with a builder, you will need to design a building plan. In the business world, a successful entrepreneur would never start a business without a business plan, so people looking to build a new home should never start that project without a good building plan.

CHAPTER 1

The single most important task in controlling your build is managing your risks. You must come up with a risk management plan to help manage the construction process from its conceptual beginnings to the closing of the home.

Risk management is the identification, analysis, monitoring, response to, and control of risks. Risks are associated with every project, including construction projects. Risks are uncertain events or conditions that, if present, can have a positive or negative affect on project objectives. Planning a risk management strategy helps mitigate the potential of negative affects during the build process. Managing your risks properly increases the probability of a timely delivery of the build and provides cost control. You need to identify all the risks, both known and unknown, and prioritize them. Once this step has been completed, define the strategies to manage these risks, including how each should be monitored to ensure compliance. In chapter 21, "Tools to Keep You in Control," you will find several spreadsheets that will help identify these risks and manage them.

Here is an example of managing your risk: financially, you have a set amount for your down payment and a certain amount for closing costs. These are known costs. But what about the unknown costs? It's not unusual for you to make changes in the house as you are advancing through the building process. As your house is constructed and you see it come together, there will be things that you will want to change. Below is a small list of five items that you will most likely want to modify in some way. These are examples of unknown costs unless you identify them and come up with a strategy to manage them.

1. Upgrading building materials (plywood versus particle board, better roofing material, stone or brick instead of vinyl siding—the list is long)
2. Adding more energy efficient windows
3. Upgrading appliances to a higher efficiency or to have stainless steel finishes
4. Changing room or window sizes
5. Moving interior walls to increase living space or bedroom space

The builder gives you a set allowance to pick out items, such as carpeting, hardwood flooring, tiles, appliances, plumbing fixtures (toilets, sinks, faucets, and tub or shower enclosures), electrical fixtures (interior, exterior lights, and doorbells) bricks, siding, cabinetry, fireplace inserts, closet shelving, and paint. Depending on your personal build, other items will fall into this category as well. These allowances vary from builder to builder, but more often than not, these allowances only cover the least expensive product on the market. The average customer will upgrade at least one or more of these items. These are **unknown costs.** When designing the new home with the architect you can have them account for these more expensive materials within the design. This allows you to control your unknown costs by handing the builder a design of the home with all the added materials built in.

Not building these added costs into the design opens the window for unknown costs to appear.

If you change designs or materials during the build, the builder will add this cost to the final bill. It is **not** unusual for the builder to show up at the closing table with a bill for these unknown costs. If the customer does not have a plan in place to track these costs, the customer is at the mercy of the builder. In most cases, the customer is under the assumption that these costs are included in the price of the build. But in most cases, the builder has the right to ask for these costs. The time to find out about any additional or unexpected costs is not at the closing table. The best way to avoid surprises at the closing table is to have a well documented and executed risk management plan that includes a change order estimate sheet (see chapter 21).

During my research, I found that some builders offer a change order process while other builders do not. They use an honor system, an old school handshake. The following is an example showing why a change order is so important.

You ask the builder if the closet can be moved to the other side of the room and made two feet longer. The builder tells you, "No problem. We will do that for you." The builder gets in touch with the rougher, who needs to order more lumber to reinforce that side of the room. The move is completed to your liking. You are under the impression that there was no extra cost involved until you hit the closing table. Now you owe the builder extra money that you did not account for. It is too late to say no to the work because the work is complete and is not reversible.

This could be a sticking point at the closing table. Either the builder needs to concede the cost, or you need to pay it. This type of situation can open up a can of worms that could have been avoided. Had there been a change order process in place, you would have known the costs up front and would have been able to make an informed decision about whether this move was worth the cost or whether you could afford to make the change.

Years ago, the handshake—a gentlemen's agreement—worked very well, but in the twenty first century, both the builder and the customer need to protect themselves from unethical people. In today's environment, it is very important that everything be put into writing and be signed by all parties involved. The change order process is a mini contract amended to the original contract. This avoids any oversights or miscommunications between the builder and customer. This process works when all parties involved sign an amendment to the original contract stating the extra work is to take place and listing the full cost of said work.

Before signing any contract with your builder, be certain a change order process is in force. If the builder does not have a change order process, it is your responsibility to let them know you have one and will enforce it throughout the build. An example of a change order process is in chapter 21. I have found that this change order is more than adequate for you to use, but as always, have your attorney review the document and put his or her seal of approval on it.

In my experience, it is well worth it to hire a real estate attorney to review all documentation and contracts. The attorney should be able to review risks that were already identified as well as cite any additional risks. Attorneys are an added expense, but they may help save time and money in the long run. They are knowledgeable about the current laws, codes, and regulations governed in your state, so they are a great asset to have on your side. The benefits of hiring an attorney well outweigh the negatives of not hiring an attorney. You will eliminate a huge risk by putting a professional on your side to help identify and remove any loopholes in contracts that may benefit the builder. If these loopholes are not identified and removed, it could leave you vulnerable and put you into a very embarrassing and costly position.

CHAPTER 2

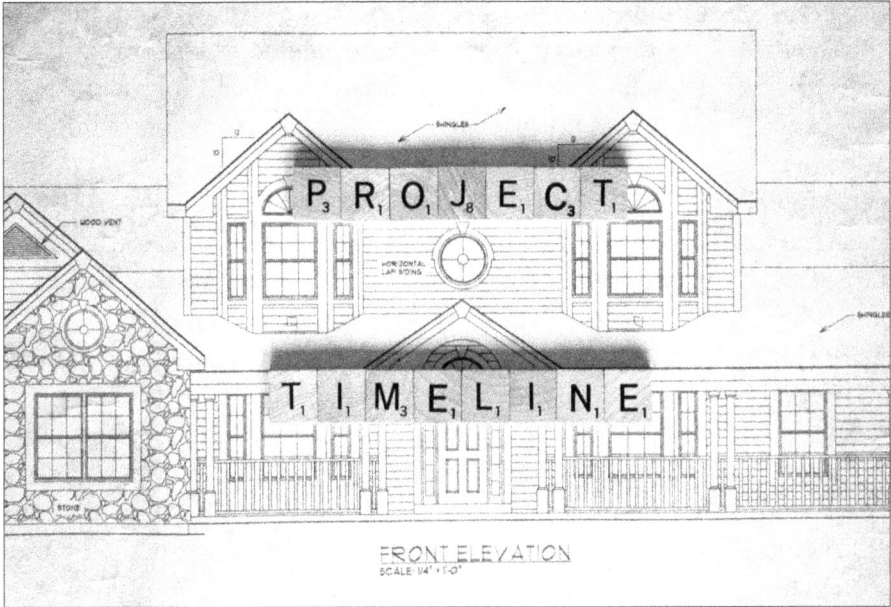

FRONT ELEVATION
SCALE: 1/4" = 1'-0"

The "PROJECT TIMELINE" or project plan is used to identify all the phases and tasks. It will show you who should be responsible for each phase and task. This is not meant to replace the builder and his responsibility, but this is a tool to help you follow along the build process and control your build. Keep in mind that timelines are always subject to change due to the nature of the business. Unexpected delays will constantly arise throughout the project. The builder can control some delays but not others. For example, an unexpected delay that the builder has little control over is extreme weather. (Snowstorms, tornados, hurricanes, and earthquakes are a few examples of extreme weather.) Weather can prevent workers from completing their work on time. Other delays are trucking delays for delivering the product and manufacturing delays due to an unexpected plant closing.

Subcontractor delays are an example of an unexpected delay that the builder does have control over. If a subcontractor is scheduled to perform his work but is seriously delayed on one or two of his previous projects and does not show up, this will most likely delays other subcontractors, who will then delay other subcontractors. This snowballs and will seriously delay the project. This is why it is critical for a builder to have a contingency plan in place to deal with these unexpected delays. You should ask the builder during your interview if they have a contingency plan. With all that being said, an example of a timeline is below. Each builder has certain timelines that work well for him. If you ask your builder, you can get a copy of his timeline.

1. **Building Permit:** The first step in the building process is to pull all necessary permits required for the build. The builder is responsible for this task. He will take the house plans to the local building department and get the house approved to be built on the land designated. After the building permit is pulled, each licensed subcontractor is required to sign off on the permit. Once again, the builder will facilitate this.

2. **Excavation:** The next step is for the builder to meet with the excavation contractor and lay out the land. This will include but is not limited to the location of the foundation, septic system, or water well if needed; utilities; driveway; and landscaping. The excavation contractor will then start.

Property excavation and rough driveway for construction equipment use

3. **Concrete Footings:** After the excavation is complete, the concrete contractor comes in next. His first job is to form and pour all piers and
footings. This is the most important job as the entire weight of the
house sits on these piers and footings. The concrete used here is different from the concrete used for the walls and any flat work, which
is why foundation walls are poured later. Most contractors will start
building the forms for the basement walls the day after the footings
are poured and pour the basement walls the day after that. There are
different variables like temperature, humidity and rain that will affect
the time frame of the next pour. Your architect will design the house in
accordance with local and state building codes. The builder will follow
the design, so there is not a lot of worry for you. Just understand that
concrete will be poured at several different times.

Concrete footings with basement walls and a stone base for concrete floor

4. **Foundation Walls:** The concrete contractor will come back after the footings are cured—sometimes as soon as the next day and sometimes as long as thirty days later. This time varies based on building codes, the weather, the temperature, and engineering designs; your builder is well aware of all variables and will keep the job on track.

5. **Waterproofing Concrete Walls:** Codes are different in all areas, but the majority of areas require that a waterproofing material be applied to the outside of the concrete. It's typically a type of tar. This procedure serves two purposes: to protect the concrete from wear and tear from water over the years and to act as a vapor barrier to help keep basements and crawlspaces dry.

Manufactured rubber waterproofing installed on outside concrete walls

Spray on waterproofing and drain piping for gutter downspouts

6. **Foundation Inspection:** In most areas, the local building code requires an inspection of the foundation. This inspection is performed to make certain the correct concrete was used and that the proper specs were followed for depth, width, and height.

7. **House Framing:** After the concrete walls are poured, the builder will determine when the framers can start building the walls using the engineering specs. The framing crew will frame and sheath the house.

House framing

8. **Rough Framing Inspection:** When the framing is completed, the building inspectors once again inspect the framework before the next phase can start.

9. **Roofing:** At this time, the finish roofing material will be installed. Doing this as soon as possible helps prevent weather damage to the sheeting.

10. **Exterior Windows and Doors:** At this time, all exterior windows and doors, including overhead garage doors, will be installed.

Exterior house wrap applied prior to window install. Window nailing strips overlap house wrap

11. **Mechanical Roughing:** After the framing, roofing, windows, and doors have been completed and inspected, the mechanics can be roughed in.

Mechanical roughing lower part of picture shows structural I beam

a. **Electrical:** All electrical panels, boxes and wiring are roughed in
    at this point. This is only the rough phase, most of this installa-
    tion are items that you will not see after the house is completed.
    The final installation of items such as outlets, switches and
    lighting will be installed at a later date.

200 amp electrical panel, the top shows the main electrical wires that supplies the power to the main breaker below that are the individual breakers that supply power throughout the house

b. **Plumbing:** All piping for the plumbing, (water, sewer and gas piping,) will be installed. The picture below shows a sample of copper and black iron piping.

Two fifty-gallon hot water heaters with natural venting

c. **HVAC:** The heating and air conditioning system will be roughed in, as will ductwork or piping for the boiler system. The picture below shows you how they can air seal the heat ducts throughout the house. Make sure you have this built into the house bid.

HVAC piping with sealant installed to prevent leakage of heating and cooling

Direct vent furnace with A/C condenser and humidifier

d. **Fireplace Roughing:** The firebox for the fireplace and chimney will be installed at this point as well as any fire or heat shields that the building department or architect have required. They will also run the gas line to the fireplaces if there is going to be a gas ignition system.

Fireplace infrastructure with fire rated drywall installed

e. **Optional Items:** Whole house vacuum, TV cable wiring, security system wiring, and surround sound wiring as well as any other item that needs to be roughed in will be done in this phase.

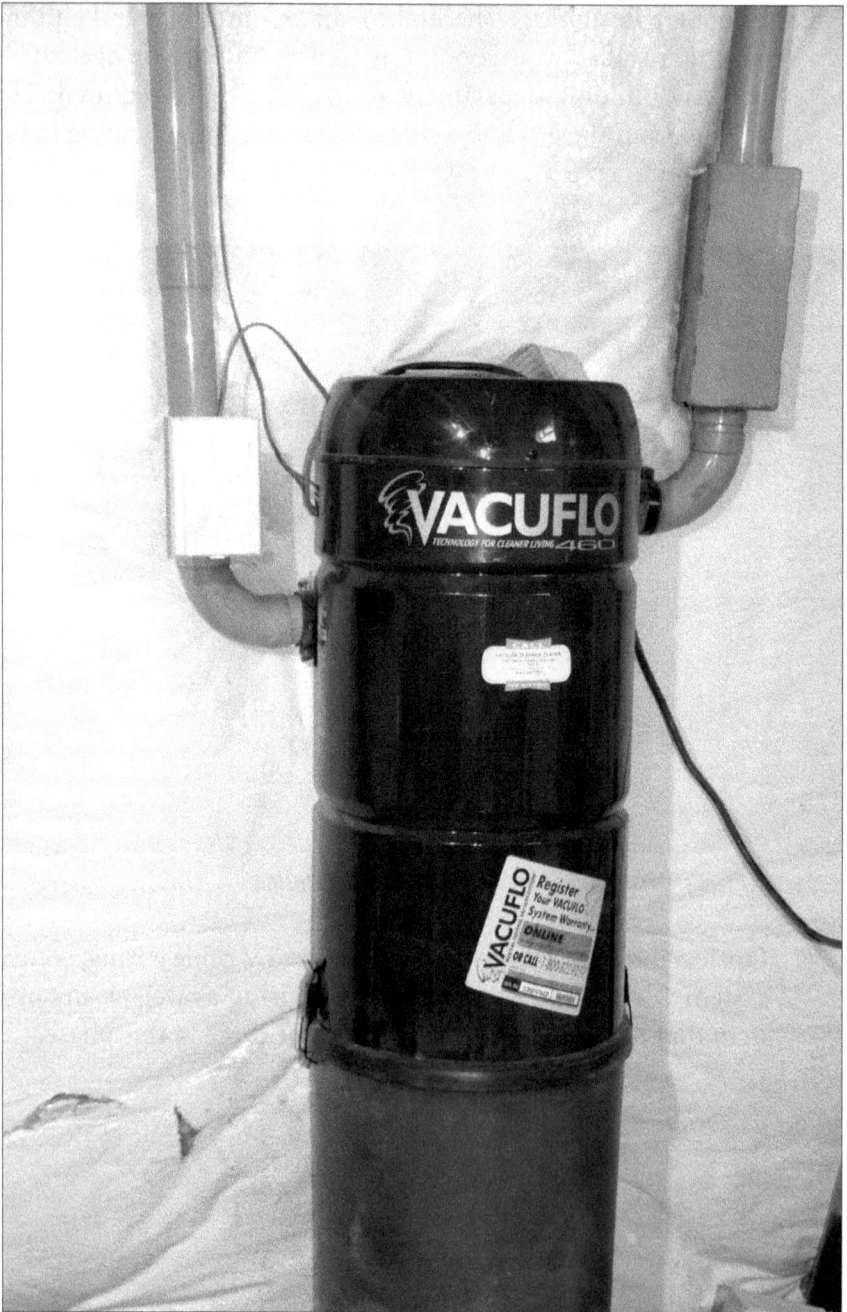

Whole house vacuum system

12. **Mechanical Inspection:** Prior to the next phase, another inspection must be performed. In most areas, several different inspectors need to come and inspect—one for electrical, one for plumbing, and the original building inspector—to make sure that any work performed did not leave the main structure weaker.

13. **Insulation:** After the framing and mechanical roughing have been completed, the contractor will contact the insulation contractor to insulate the house.

14. **Insulation Inspection:** The inspectors need to come back at this point to make sure the insulation has been installed correctly.

15. **Interior Walls:** After the insulation inspections are complete, the builder will contact the drywall contractor. The drywall contractor's first task is to have all the drywall delivered to the job site and put inside each room for installation. The drywall contractor can now install and finish all interior walls.

16. **Exterior:** Most contractors wait until the drywall is at least delivered to the inside of the building and the roof is installed before they start installing any of the exterior cover. They wait because the weight of the roof and drywall help the house settle. If the exterior is installed prior to the drywall delivery and roof installation, the house might settle enough to make the siding or brickwork buckle. So, the exterior can be started while the interior walls are installed and finished.

17. **Painting:** After the interior walls are hung and finished, the painting crew comes in and starts the painting process. The first phase of painting is to prime all drywall; the second phase is to paint all ceilingsl and the third phase is to paint all walls the specified colors. At that point, if the builder has had all the trim and interior doors delivered to the site, they can start the fourth phase: priming and painting all the windows, doors, and trim with the first and second coats of paint. After all interior work is completed and just before the final walkthrough, the painters will come back and do any touch up painting needed.

18. **Interior Trim Work:** At this point, the carpenters can come in and complete any trim work, such as around doors, windows, stair railings, and any handcrafted cabinetry.

19. **Cabinetry Installation:** After the painting is complete, the cabinetry can be installed. This includes but is not limited to the kitchen, bathroom, and office.

20. **Countertop Installation:** After the cabinetry has been installed, the countertops in all areas of the house can now be installed.

21. **All Tile Work:** All tile work can be completed at this time. This includes but is not limited to the shower and bathtub walls, kitchen and bathroom backsplashes, and flooring.

22. **Mechanical Finish:** After the painting is complete and the cabinetry is installed, the mechanicals can be finished: electrical, plumbing, HVAC, and any other optional items (security system, central vacuum, and surround sound). Some of this finish work can be completed prior to or at the same time as the cabinetry being installed.

23. **Interior Flooring:** After the cabinetry is installed and the majority of the mechanics are finished, the flooring will be installed. The reason I say "the majority of the mechanicals" is that some of the mechanics require flooring in order to be installed.

24. **Driveways and Walkways:** After the exterior of the house is complete, the builder will have the driveways and walkways installed.

Concrete driveway and side walks installed before final lanscaping

25. **Landscaping:** After the driveways and sidewalks are installed, the final landscaping can be performed. This can be a very expensive project, so make sure you have enough in your budget to complete it.

Completed exterior landscaping

26. **Finalizing the Interior:** After the flooring and mechanics are complete, the final touches can be performed, such as closet shelving, mirrors, and any other odds and ends that are required.

27. **Final Drywall and Painting (including touch up painting):** At this point, the builder is getting ready to close on the house and hand over the keys to the new owner. He has the drywall company and the painters come back in for the final touch ups. During the final stages of interior installations, sometimes walls are dinged and or the paint gets scuffed up. This is step is performed so that the house is perfect for the new homeowners.

28. **Final Cleanup:** After the final touches are complete, the last step before final inspection is to have cleaners come in and clean. The builder should have the cleaners clean everything, from the outside siding and concrete to the interior windows and appliances. This is an item you may want to cover during negotiations, so make it clear how the house should be on closing day.

29. **Final Inspection:** After all work has been complete, the building inspectors need to perform a final inspection and issue a Certificate of Occupancy (CO). This allows the builder and owner to close on the house and the property to be occupied.

30. **New Owner Walk through:** At this point, after the final inspection is complete, the house passes, and the cleaning crew has completely cleaned everything. The builder and the new owner get together to do the final walk through. This is your time to make sure everything is working and that the house is ready for you to live in. If there are items to be completed, make certain the builder addresses them. Once the house is signed over to the new owner, all work should be complete. The only work that should be performed after that day is warrantee work. Everything else should have been done before closing.

CHAPTER 3

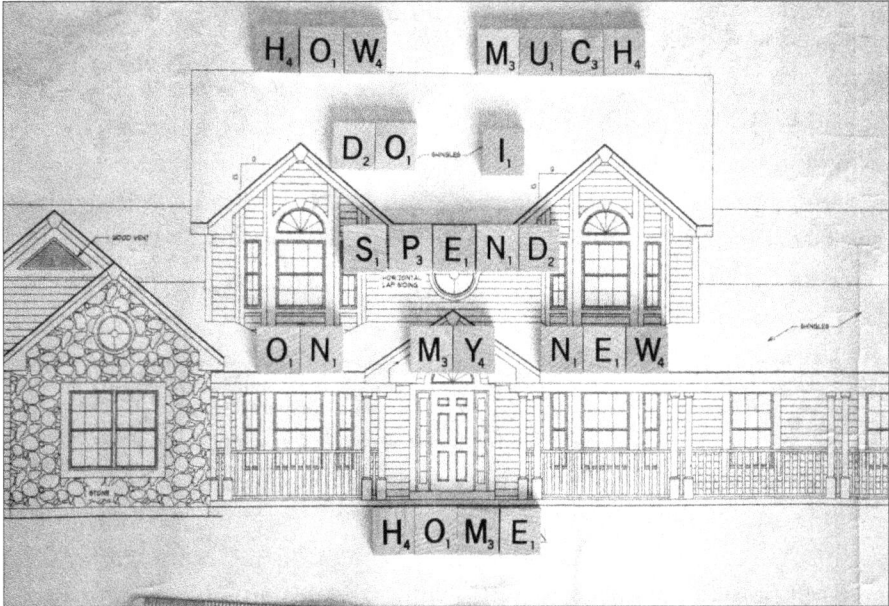

In this chapter, I will address something that you probably have already given a great deal of thought about: How much money should you spend on your new home? This is a very complex question but is ultimately the most important step in building your dream home. There is nothing worse than building the perfect home only to find out you can't afford it. The US economy changed drastically in 2006 when housing prices reached their peak and started to decline later that year. Homeowners began to feel the pinch. Many homeowners were given too much financing on their houses. This created an unprecedented amount of foreclosures, and hardworking Americans lost their American dream. That being said, you are the only person who knows how much money you can afford or are willing to invest in your new home. After what has happened in the last ten years with the housing bust, banks have changed their lending practices but still seem to lend a little bit more than the homeowner can actually afford. You need to take this question very seriously and not put yourself in a position where you work long and hard to build your dream home only to find out that you cannot afford it!

Below are eight steps that will help reveal how much you can afford. My best advice would be to get yourself a note book and title it "How Much Do I Spend On My New Home". Use this notebook to write each step down, as you discover new answers insert them under the respective step. I have always found that writing things down helps me with two things, the first thing is to not forget anything and the second is it allows me to sleep better knowing that if I wrote it down I will not forget about it. If you have another idea that works good for you use it but either way, do yourself a favor and use something. It will help in the decision making process.

Step 1: How much money can you afford to pay each month?

Start by setting up a meeting with your financial advisor and/or accountant. They are professionals familiar with your finances. This could be a big help in determining how much money you can afford each month. Keep in mind that you are moving to a new location and a new house, so this will undoubtedly change your entire budget. Do not cut yourself short of money for things you may want to do after you move into your new home. This is addressed in more detail in chapter 10.

The following is a list of items that will most likely change from your current household budget. You will need to compile your own list and look at each one to come up with an estimated cost associated with each item on the list. Keep in mind that these factors will vary, depending on the size and location of your new house and the energy efficiency of your old versus your new home.

a. Electric bill.
b. Garbage pickup.
c. HVAC bill (natural gas, propane, electric, or other sources of energy).
d. Vehicle bills can change based on your commute to and from work. (Tires, gas, oil change, and vehicle replacement.)
e. House maintenance: if your new home is bigger, the bills may very well increase accordingly (cleaning, lawn cutting, and snow removal, watering the lawn and gardening).

f. Property taxes.
g. Homeowners insurance.
h. Flood insurance, if required. (You need to do research to see if flood insurance is required for your new property.)
i. Development or association fees.
j. Interest rates on home loan.

Step 2: Get an idea of what size home and location you think would suit your family's needs.
Go to some open houses in the same area you are looking to build. Speak to either the real estate agent or homeowner(s) and ask to see the past utility bills. Keep in mind that if the house is brand new, they will not have the information. If the house is too old, the utilities could be off due to modern technology (energy efficient windows, doors, insulation, etc.) Try to find homes up to five years old.

Step 3: Are you selling a house?
If you do not have a home to sell, skip this step and go to step 4. If you are selling an existing home, more information on this topic is in the next chapter.

Step 4: Set up a meeting with your financial institution.
You need to figure out the term for the loan you want. This will allow you to get the interest rate for that length of time. (Keep in mind that interest rates do change daily until you lock the rate in, and this could effect your payment.)Your financial institution can tell you how much your payment will be per every thousand dollars borrowed; keep in mind this figure is for principal and interest only.

Your taxes and homeowners insurance will be in addition to these figures and will vary from town to town. You can contact the town assessors' office to get an idea about what the tax base is for local and school taxes. (If there is a loan on the property, the lending institution will most likely hold an escrow account. They will add the yearly taxes and insurance, divide by twelve payments, and add it to your monthly payment. They will pay the taxes and insurance when due. This allows them to protect their investment.)

Another cost could be principal mortgage insurance (PMI). This protects the bank if the borrower defaults on the loan and borrowed more than what the bank could recoup after selling and closing cost. Check with your bank about what the requirements are. Typically, PMI will not be required when you have a 20 percent down payment. The financial institution can also give you an idea about how much your closing cost will be, minus your attorney fees.

I recommend being preapproved for a mortgage. This will allow you to better utilize your time and not spin your wheels. This could be a huge negotiating chip while shopping for a builder.

Step 5: Set up an appointment with your insurance agent.
At this point, you will not be able to get an exact quote because you have not decided exactly what size home you are building, but you can get a ballpark figure. A local insurance agent could very well know what areas would require specialty insurance. If not, a call to your local town building department will help you with these answers.

Step 6: Call the local assessor's office.
They can give you the price per thousand dollars of assessed value for taxes. Again, this is going to be a ballpark amount until you choose an exact size home and location.

Step 7: Make an appointment with your attorney.
Find out what his or her costs will be for reviewing your building plans and contracts as well as closing costs. (Keep in mind paying an attorney to review a contract is well worth the cost. DO NOT SIGN ANYTHING WITHOUT HIS OR HER APPROVAL.)

Step 8: Review the information.
After the completion of steps one through six, you should have enough information to help you make a decision about how much to spend on your new home.

CHAPTER 4

The following is a list of several ways to sell your home. In addition to this list, you may uncover other ways through your own research as well as through family, friends, or neighbors. Research all the options and make the right choice for your personal situation.

The most important thing to remember regardless of which option you choose is that you can always come down in price for your home but generally (unless there is a bidding war) you cannot go up in price. If you have time to wait, you should price your home high. You can always lower the price if there is no activity. If you are in a hurry, you need to make sure the house is priced right with a couple things to keep in mind. You don't want to leave any money on the table but need it priced to sell quickly.

Below are four different options that I am aware of that you can use to sell your house.

1. Traditional Realty Companies

Having time to show your house to prospective customers is imperative. If you do not have the time, using a traditional Realtor will be your best way to go. This option will cost you the most money, but it is worth it if you do not have the time or any sales experience. The realty company receives a percentage of the selling price. The ballpark is 6 percent to 8 percent of the selling price. The listing agent gets 3 percent to 4 percent just for signing your house on the market, and the selling agent gets the other 3 percent to 4 percent. I have seen where realty agents run around and list more houses than they can service. This happened to me where the realtor was in a hurry to list my house then after I signed the contract I never really saw him again. He promised he would have open houses and work hard on selling my house. After 3 months, I dropped the listing with him. Lessons learned show how picking the right agent is very important.

I have sold two homes through a Realtor. One of them was bad. The agent put my house on the market and that was the last day I saw him. He was lazy and could not have cared less who sold the house because he knew he was getting his commission. He promised to have an open house and advertise the house in the local paper—neither of which he did. The other Realtor was awesome. I had an agent who worked his tail off to list and sell the house. I wish I had used him both times but chalk it up to lessons learned.

When you sign up to have an agent list your house, you have to sign a contract with the agency. The contract locks you in for a certain amount of time. If you pick an agency that you are not happy with, you are stuck for the duration of the contract. After you have signed the contract, if, you choose to sell on your own or change agents, the only way out is to take the house off the market until the specified time listed in the agreement has lapsed. So if you choose this option, do your homework before you sign anything, and always have your attorney review any contracts before you sign.

You may know someone who used this approach and was very happy with the results. Referrals are **sometimes** your best way of finding a good agent. Make sure you find an agent with your best interest in mind—not his or her paycheck, at the cost of your profit. Do not feel obligated to take the first agent you speak to. Let the agents know you are researching all your options and that you will get back to them. Interview several agents and have each one tell you what the house should be listed for. Also, ask each agent for a list of references and make sure you call each one. Ask them many questions, especially about things that are important to you. Real estate fees differ from area to area. You pay nothing up front, but you pay a percentage of the sale on closing day.

2. Seller Assisted Real Estate Companies

Using this option does require more of your time. If you have the time to answer calls, set up and have private viewings, and set up and run the open house on weekends, this might be the way to go.

Some realty companies will provide a program that allows you to sell your home on your own but not alone. The seller assisted program is a way for you to save thousands of dollars selling your house. Here is how it works. There is an up front cost of anywhere from $499.00 to $999.00. This cost includes, listing your house on the Multiple Listing Service (MLS). The MLS system is a powerful tool that allows all realtors to find your house as well as prospective homebuyers. They also give you For Sale and Open House signs, run ads in the local paper, supply you with a highlight sheet (detailed information about your property), and assist you with paperwork to accept an offer. You pay no commission if *you* sell the house without an agent. If you accept an offer from a licensed real estate agent, there will be a 2 percent to 4 percent commission paid out of the sale price. Whether you sell it yourself or an agent sells your house, you will save a substantial amount of money versus the traditional realty company.

3. Professional Flat Fee, Noncommission Real Estate Companies

The third way to sell your home is with help from an agency that never charges a commission. If you are in a hot area where houses sell very quickly then this might be the way to go. If houses sell slowly in your area then this might not be the way to go. They do not list your house on the MLS so prospective buyers may never even see that your house is for sale. This program will cost anywhere from $400.00 to $900.00. They give you all the material to list your house: For Sale and Open House signs, brochures, highlight sheets, and paperwork to help you accept offers. They advertise your house through their own websites and local newspapers, and in most cases, they have their own papers. There are no real estate agents involved, and there is never a commission. You play a role in your real estate sale process to the entire market of potential homebuyers. To ensure your success, you will meet with one of their professionally trained consultants who will thoroughly discuss the process of selling your home and answer any questions you may have. They will also be available throughout the entire process should any questions arise.

4.   Home For Sale by Owner

The fourth way to sell your house is to sell it on your own with no help from anyone. There is the cost of you coming up with signs and brochures and running ads in the newspaper and Internet yourself. This could get costly if the house is on the market for a long time. The exception to this would be if the house were located in high demand area and/or very visible area where many people can see the signs. In this case, the house could sell very quickly without having to run many newspaper and Internet ads. This would be the recommended way to go because you would save the most money.

My recommendation is simple: do not throw yourself into a situation until you have clearly defined every aspect and requirement involved with a construction build. Bottom line: one must do one's homework. Identify all the risks, analyze/prioritize them, and make informed decisions. Again, it is up to you to perform your due diligence to find the best way for you to sell your house.

CHAPTER 5

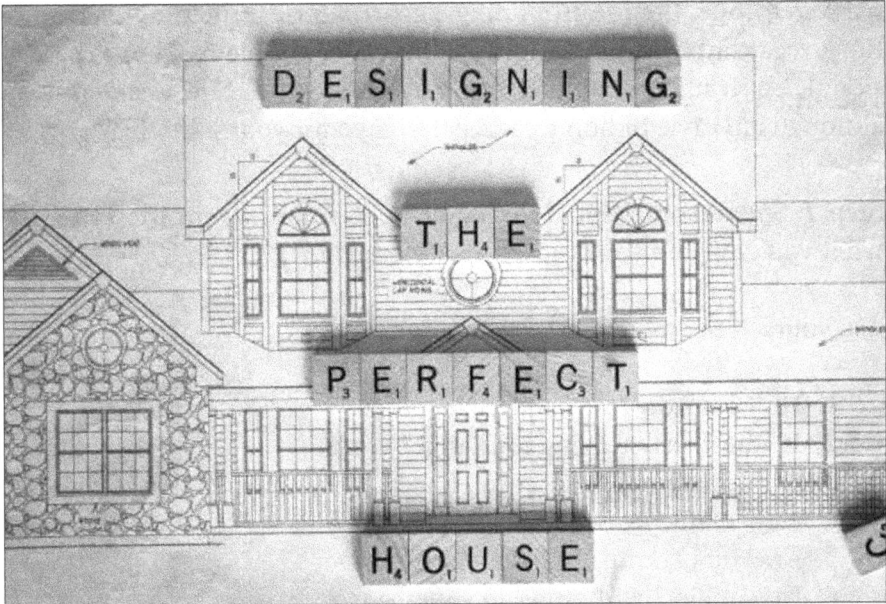

DESIGNING THE PERFECT HOUSE

Every person has different tastes; open your mind and let your ideas come out. Keep in mind that all builders have a preferred house they like to build, but they will build any style of house that you want. Just because you do not see a particular style of home that you like through a builder does not mean it cannot be built for you. Do not let anyone tell you that a house is perfect for you when you know deep down it is not. When you see the perfect house, you will know it. We will cover selecting the right builder in chapter 8. The key to knowing what kind of house you should build is to keep an open mind and be diligent. Spend a lot of time on step 4.

Below you will find steps to help you make this very important decision.

Step 1: What hemisphere do you live in?
Each hemisphere has different weather factors that need to be considered prior to selecting your style of home. Weather will make a huge

difference in what kind of house you will need to build. Builders and their engineers are very familiar with what the local and state building codes are, so when you speak to them, they can give you ideas. As a third party resource, the local building department can help answer questions regarding weather factors for your area. While making this decision, keep in mind certain homes fare better in certain weather areas, although any style of home can be designed for your particular area.

Step 2: Spend some time looking at both your current lifestyles and what you envision your future lifestyle to be.

Ask yourself the following questions.

1. How long do you plan to live there?
2. Is your lifestyle going to change? Why?
3. How many children do you have?
4. How many bedrooms do you need?
5. Are you planning to have more children?
6. How many bedrooms will you need?
7. Do you have children living out of town? Will they be staying with you when they visit?
8. Do you have other relatives living out of town? Will they stay with you when they visit?
9. Do you or family members currently have a handicap or could in the future? Do you need handicapped access?
10. When you advance to retirement years, do you want to climb stairs?
11. Do you like to entertain?

    a. Do you want a finished basement? Keep in mind that some towns require one to two additional egresses (exits) from the basement if a living area is to be built. A visit or phone call to the local building department will help answer this question. These egresses could be either a stairway or a window well.

b. Do you need a larger family room?

c. Do you want open floor plans, where you can utilize several rooms that flow together?

12. Do you like to cook in or eat out more?

a. Do you want a bigger kitchen or a smaller one?

b. Do you need more cupboard space?

c. Do you need a larger pantry space?

13. How many vehicles do you have?

a. Do you like to park them inside or out?

b. Do you like to work out of the garage or shed? Keep in mind that some developments do not allow sheds. If a shed is what you are looking to have, made certain you can build one.

14. Do you currently work out of your home or will you in the future?

a. Do you need a big or small office?

b. Will you have clients visiting? Do you want outside access to the office?

    i) What special equipment does your home based business need to function?

    ii) Does this require special wiring?

Step 3: Make sure you write down all your answers.

In chapter 21 "Tools to keep you in control", you will find helpful spreadsheets to use. You will also find those sheets and more on my web site WWW.controlyourbuild.com click on the "Tools" tab and type in user name and password.

User name: controlyourbuild
Password: tools

You can also design your own whichever way you choose it is important to write them down somewhere. Keeping them in your head will only confuse you and keep you up at night. After you have answered the above questions, keep them handy, as you may want to make changes. Sharing them with the builder prior to design will help with any oversights.

Step 4: Options for researching home types and styles in your area.

1. Visit many open houses.
2. Researching homes that are no more than five years old will prove to be most effective.
3. Speak to the homeowners directly (Realtors are looking to sell).
   a. Ask the homeowners what they like or dislike about the home.
   b. What would they have done differently?
4. Visit new build home shows.
5. Magazines on new homes are very helpful.
6. Visit local lumber stores for new home construction or design books.
7. The Internet has many sites for new home construction.
8. Contact local architects and find out what they have to offer.

CHAPTER 6

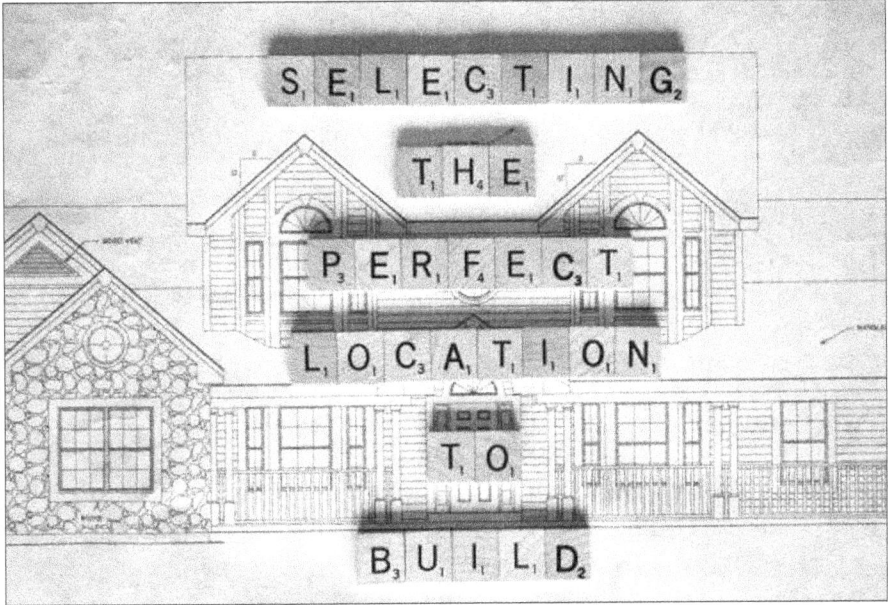

Where do I build? This is a very important question. When someone is looking to build a dream home, the location of the build is crucial. The answer to this question is with you and your family members. The first thing you need to do is sit down and spend some time with the family members who will be affected by the new house. Discuss and answer the following questions.

1. **Commute to work:**

   a. Do I need easy access to a thruway?
   b. Where does the family work? How long of a commute do we have now, and how long of a commute do we want in the future? Do we want to drive to work or take public transportation to work?

   c. Mileage, with the ever rising price of gas, is a consideration. How far is too far to drive to work?

   d. Are carpooling and public transportation offered around the new location?

2. Local school system:

   a. Are you looking for a new school, or do you want to stay in an existing school?

   b. How are the schools rated in the area?

   c. Is it a growing school system?

   d. School taxes could change, depending on the growth of schools.

   e. Consider public schools verses private schools in the area.

3. Lifestyle:

   a. Do you want to live near or away from family?

   b. Do you have elderly parents who may need your help down the road? Maybe you will need to design the house where you can add an in law apartment.

4. Weather conditions to consider:

   a. Hurricane zones

   b. Tornado alley

   c. Flood zones

   d. Snow belt

5. Do you want your house in the sun or shade and at what times of day?

   a. Which direction do you want your house facing? This will affect whether the morning sun shines on the deck/patio in the morning or afternoon. If you are in an area with tough winters, which way does the wind blow?

   b. Will the snow drift heavily in the driveway?

c. Do you like to watch TV in the evening? Is the TV room in the back, where the sun will shine and create glare when you are trying to watch TV?

d. What kind of landscaping do you want to put in? Does it require morning sun or afternoon sun?

6. Noise pollution:

Local noise changes from day to night and from weekday to weekends, so when you visit the area, make sure you visit during all different times. This will require several visits. There are a few variables listed below to keep in mind:

a. What is your work schedule like? Do you work during the week or on weekends, days, or night? Will daytime noise affect your sleep?

b. Is there a thruway or state highway nearby?

c. Is there an airport nearby?

d. Are there farms or a commercial property nearby?

e. How far is the potential location from an industrial property? Keep in mind that land could be developed down the road, depending on how the property is zoned, which determines what could be built there. A visit to the local zoning office could be helpful.

f. Are there train tracks nearby?

CHAPTER 7

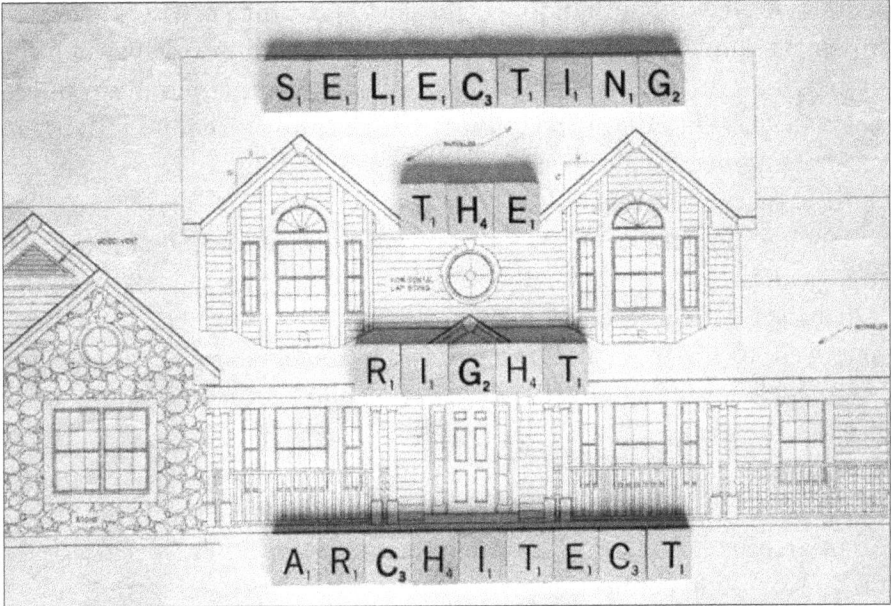

"Selecting The Right Architect" can save a homeowner a considerable amount of money. This chapter will help you understand this concept. When a house is designed, much thought goes into helping the builders and developers mass produce a development. The homes within most developments are designed with the option to make a few changes, but all homes within the development are essentially the same. The builder will have a list of the vendors and materials that you can choose from to help you customize the home within their guidelines. If you are building this house in a development and you want to make changes to the house design they're offering, it could get costly as the house was designed to follow certain design patterns.

The only cost effective way to save money while designing a home to your liking is to hire an architect. Architects will help you design the house of your dreams, keeping material waste to a minimum while maintaining all building codes and regulations. If you decide to buy a piece of land outside of a development, the architect can save you money by helping you design the house to suit the property, including any wells, septic systems, and outbuildings. The laws regarding engineering design for single family homes vary from state to state, but normally when the design of a structural element is not prescribed in the applicable residential code (i.e., an LVL or steel beam), the engineer is required to design it. That engineer might work for the owner, the builder, or the supplier of the structural element.

An engineering stamp on a drawing simply indicates that the drawing was drawn by or under the direct supervision of the engineer and that he/she is registered in the state shown on the stamp. If an engineer were to stamp an architect's drawing, the engineer would become responsible for the architect's work, so it would be rare unless they work in the same firm.

The structural drawings for a building are normally on separate sheets and are more diagrammatic than the representative drawings of an architect. The drawings might also contain notes, specifications, dimensions, and connection details.

The architectural drawings also show those structural elements, but there is usually a note referring the builder to the structural drawings for the actual sizes. Showing the sizes of structural members in more than one place in a drawing set is normally avoided.

Building elements that need no engineering design (such as structural elements prescribed in the building code) are usually described in the architect's drawings and specifications. You do not need to get into all the details of this because among your attorneys, the building department, the builder, and the architect or engineer, it is more likely that all plans are properly stamped.

If you want your house to look different from every other house in the area, hiring a professional to design the home is the way to go. You need to start with finding an architect or engineer who works within your area. Building codes vary from town to town, state to state, and region to region. There are many different reasons each area has different building codes. Below is a list of some of the reasons, but it is not an inclusive list.

1. Snow load zones.
2. Soil conditions.
3. Flood zones.
4. Earthquake zones.
5. Hurricane zones.
6. Areas prone to tornados.
7. Extremely hot areas.
8. Extremely cold areas.
9. Extreme high wind area.
10. Water supply: public water or well.
11. Areas that have no public sewer system

Other factors need to be considered that could impact the cost of a build. Building material supply chains is one factor that could adversely affect cost. Every area has different type of building materials that are prevalent to that particular region. Having these types of materials transported from one area to another will raise the cost of said material. The architect designs homes with this in mind. This does not mean you cannot get whatever material you desire. It just means that it is going to affect the cost.

With all that being said, selecting an architect is an important factor in saving time and money. There are several ways to select the right architect. Like always, do your homework and research all options, such as:

1. Contacting your local building department is a good start and find out if the architect has had any negligent law suit or if he has a history of questionable designs.

2. Contact local builders and find out whom they use for an architect and how easy they are to work with.

3. Visit your local lumber stores talk to the sales department and see whom they recommend.

4. Online research can uncover a lot of good and bad. Just keep in mind there are always people that can never be pleased. Do not just take one or two reviews, look at all the reviews you can find.

5. Better Business Bureau can be another good source although use this source in conjunction with other sources.

6. Contact your state and county licensing agencies to find out if the architect is in good standing and has all the appropriate licenses required.

7. Spend sometime talking with relatives, friends, coworkers, and neighbors; sometimes this is the best source when trying to find a good business. During this search, it will also uncover the bad business.

On my web site under the "Tools" tab (see chapter 21 for web site and log in information) you will find a spreadsheet labeled "Selecting the Right Architect." Use this sheet to compile a list of architects you are interested in. I recommend you find at least twelve or so to compare against each other. Keeping track on paper will allow you to see your research in black and white and allow you to make an educated selection. Once you have narrowed your search down to the twelve or so, you will need to reach out and speak with them. Below is a list of questions you should find out to help you make a decision.

1. How long has the architect been in business? This is up to your comfort level my comfort level is 10 years or more.

2. Has the architect ever been sued for items related to designing homes? For me it depends on the type of suit, if the architect was convicted of negligence then I think I would have to eliminate that architect from the list.

3. What percent of residential versus commercial does the architect design? I suggest finding one that strictly does residential.

4. How many homes has the architect designed? The more the better but I feel twenty within the past ten years is a good number.

5. What is the average square footage of the homes the architect designed? You do not want to hire an architect that only designs small homes if you are looking to build a large home or an architect that only designs large homes if you are looking to build a small home. I feel that if the architect's average square footage of designed homes were with in one to two thousand square feet of the size you are looking to build that would be optimal.

6. Where are the homes located that the architect designed? This will allow you to visit these areas and look at the homes he has designed.

7. Is the architect insured? You want to make sure that they all the proper insurance. If you contact the local building department, insurance companies and your attorney, they should be able to help with how much insurance the architect should carry.

8. How does the architect charge for designing a residential structure? Does the architect charge by the hour, square foot, or both? Remember you are going to have a budget to stay within so make sure that you can afford them. Keep in mind the more complex the design the more expensive it is going to be.

9. What is the average time from start to stamped blueprints? Only you know what your timeframe is for this project just be certain they can design your dream home within your allotted timeframe.

CHAPTER 8

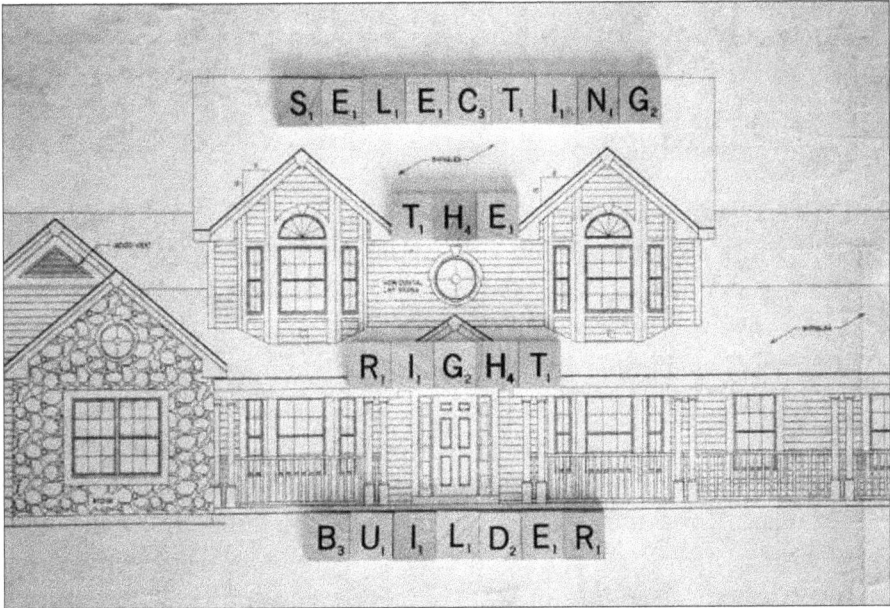

Selecting the right builder will ultimately be the most important task you do. If you select the right builder, you will be heading in the right direction, but if you select the wrong builder, it could be very bad. With the wrong builder, you will run into many problems not only for the short term but also possibly for the rest of your life. Attention to detail is the name of this game. You should select a builder based on certain factors, and money should be one of the least important. I recommend following the list below. This will help you narrow your search down to three to five builders that you are comfortable with. Good luck and don't forget do your homework!

1. Before you start, get yourself a nice big binder and a pen, bring the binder and pen with you everywhere you go. You will find out along the way that you will uncover information about a builder in places

that you were not expecting. Always ask many questions and write the answers down. You will be surprised how much information you forgot while reviewing your notes.

2. Personality is very important; you will need to make sure you can work together with the builder and employees of the company. This will be a long project, and you will be talking with the builder and his employees on a daily basis.

3. Contact your local Better Business Bureau (BBB). Keep in mind this is just a starting point, not a final decision maker. A consumer can file a complaint against a particular business through the BBB. The consumer submits a complaint and details how they feel they were mistreated. After receiving a complaint, the BBB will contact the business in question to get the other side of the complaint. The BBB acts as a liaison. When calling, you will need to find out how many complaints customer have made against the builder, and out of those complaints how many have been resolved. If a builder has built a lot of homes then there is a good chance there are at least some complaints made, keep in mind that sometimes customers will jump the gun and call to complain about a business for something that turned out to be simply a misunderstanding. If complaints were resolved in a timely manner then that says a lot about the builder, it shows that he cares about his reputation. To get deeper you can also find out what the complaint was and see what the builder did to make sure the customer was completely satisfied.

4. The local chamber of commerce is another source to contact. When contacting the chamber of commerce, ask the same questions as you did when you contacted the Better Business Bureau.

5. Drive through a development where the builder has built new homes. Stop and ask homeowners if they had the builder build for them and start asking questions.

   a. How was the builder to work with?
   b. How is the quality of their home now?

    c. How is the house holding up against time?

    d. Did the builder stop back the following year to follow up?

    e. Was the builder on time with the build?

    f. Do they know other homeowners who used the same builder?

    g. If they were to do it all over again, would they have used the same builder?

    h. If the answer above is no, whom would they rather have gone with and why?

Do not forget to bring a camera, your binder and pen with you. Keep track of all questions asked and all answers given. You will find that when you start asking around, many people are willing to give you advice, good and bad. Writing things down will help you stay organized and keep you from getting confused.

6. Ask the builder to supply you with a list of references. Call all of them and ask questions. These calls may lead you to unhappy customers, if any. Keep in mind that the builder will never give you a reference for someone who was unhappy. It is your job to find out if there are any out there.

7. Most builders have a manager who takes care of day to day onsite management as well as an office manager who takes care of the behind the scene events, billing, permit change orders, and so on. Find out from the builder who these people are. Ask the builder if you can meet them. Meeting these managers will give you an opportunity to see if there could be any personality conflicts. You will most likely spend time sorting items out with these two managers.

8. Find out what the chain of command is. This step is important because throughout the build, if there are any questions or problems that arise, you will need to know whom to call and who has the power to make decisions.

9. Your local building department may be another source for finding out how the builder does work. Again, ask many questions. Keep in

mind that it is not legal or ethical for a government office to steer you toward or away from a particular business. As you ask questions, you will get a feel for how a builder does work.

10. Insert your notes into the spreadsheet included in chapter 21. This will help you see patterns for each builder; these patterns will help you select the best three to five builders.

11. After you have selected three to five builders, work with these builders to help design the perfect home. You will find that each builder has different ideas; you will want to use these ideas in your new home.

12. Before you get into the negotiations with the builders, it is very important to have the home you want broken down in detail. When it comes down to picking out your lighting fixtures, plumbing fixtures, cabinets, appliances, and flooring, builders will give you a list of suppliers to pick from. They will then give you an allowance to pick these items. I have found that some builders will not give you enough allowance to pick out what you want, and then you start running into unknown expenses. This is why it is important to find out what your allowance will be for each item. Make sure your budget has enough wiggle room to cover the building products you want.

13. After you have designed the home of your dreams, have your three to five builders bid on the house. There is an old saying about apples and oranges. It is very important to have each builder bid on the same specs so you can compare apples against apples and oranges against oranges.

14. Before you sign the final contract with the builder, check off the following.

    a. Did your attorney review the contract and approve it?

    b. Did you review the final pricing with your bank or accountant to make certain you can afford what you just designed?

     c.   Can the builder complete the job in your specified timeframe?

     d.   Does your gut tell you that this is the correct builder?

15. If you feel that you have successfully completed this chapter, you are ready for the next chapter.

CHAPTER 9

It is very important to successfully complete the prior chapter before meeting with the builder. This will give you the extra negotiating power you need to save money. The way this economy has been, builders are hungry to build homes. The negotiation will move along quite well if you are prepared by doing your homework.

You can save a lot of money during the negotiation. The builder does not want to leave any money on the table. Your thought should be that the more money the builder leaves on the table, the more money you could put back into your wallet. Let me explain that for a moment. The builder comes to the meeting not knowing what other prices you have received from other builders. The builder will try to get that information out of you. Do yourself a favor and do not tip the scale in his or her favor. The less you talk about what other builders have told you, the better off you are.

Keep the conversation focused on what you want and what the builder can offer you. Keep in mind you need to let each builder know exactly what you want, including what type of materials you request. Be very up front and honest. This allows you to compare apples to apples and oranges to oranges as discussed in the previous chapter. Make sure you review all work to be completed as well as the type of material to be used. Builders can change the types of material used to give the appearance of a less expensive bid. (An example is that oriented strand board is less expensive than real plywood, so if a builder were to use it in the bid, the bid would appear to be less expensive than a bid using real plywood.) If the builder does this throughout the entire house, the bid could be quite a bit less expensive on paper, but unfortunately, by the time the certificate of occupancy is issued and the homeowner is sitting at the closing table, the cost of build the house has exceeded the expectations.

The simple way to control your build and save money is to do the research to know exactly what you want in your house. It is very time consuming but well worth it in the end. Below is a list of items that need to be researched. The level of quality needs to be decided prior to signing with a builder. Each item below is covered in more detail throughout book.

1. Location of house, including which direction you want your house facing: north, south, east, or west. (Do you like more sun in the a.m. or p.m?)

2. Square footage of house desired, including square footage of living space versus square footage of closet/pantry space.

3. The type and quality of shelving in closets and pantry.

4. Quantity of bedrooms desired. (Do you want more bedrooms or fewer bedrooms with more square footage per bedroom?)

5. Quality and type of material used for each bedroom including but not limited to type of flooring (carpet or hardwoods; high end or low end), lighting fixtures (recessed or hanging), ceiling style (flat, trayed,

cathedral, or shed style), and paint (quality, color, and sheen) in each bedroom.

6. Quantity of bathrooms desired, including whether it will be a full, three quarter, or half bath.

7. Quality and type of materials used for bathrooms, including but not limited to bathtubs (standard, claw foot, oversized, or whirlpool), showers (standard, multiple showerheads, and stand up or sit down bench), sinks (single or double), cabinetry (high or low profile, color, style, and type of material), toilets (high or low profile, color, and style), lighting fixtures (recessed, hanging, oversized, and quality), mirrors (large, small, fixed, or recessed), and flooring (carpet, tile, or hardwood, including heated).

8. Kitchen size. Do you like to entertain or cook a lot? Do you have or plan to have a large family?

9. Quality and quantity of kitchen cabinets and pantry size. Cabinetry comes in several sizes and varying material quality. This can alter the cost of the home by several thousand dollars. Countertops also come in different materials (Formica, stone, granite, marble, and wood), and the cost can vary by several thousands of dollars.

10. Kitchen appliances. Do you want standard appliances or commercial grade?

11. Entertainment room. Do you need more than just one or two rooms? Do you want a family room and a sitting room or just one large great room?

12. Dining room. Do you need a separate dining room or is a large eating area attached to the kitchen good enough?

13. Fireplaces. Do you need or desire one? Is more than one desired (in the family room, sitting room, dining room, and bedroom)? Does the fireplace need to be wood burning, gas logs, or a fireplace insert?

What size fireplace would you prefer? Do you want a mantle for the fireplace or a flat front? Do you want tile or marble surrounding it?

14. Heating and air conditioning. Do you desire one or two systems? Is the system going to be high efficiency or standard? Is it a forced air system or a boiler system with radiant heat? Do you need or desire separate zones in the house so that you can turn the heat up or down or air condition different areas of house depending on time of day or night?

15. Garage or carport? Do you want it attached or detached? Front load or side load? What size (single car garage, double car garage, or larger)? Do you have large vehicles that require higher garage doors? Do you want two single garage doors or one double garage door? There are also man doors in garages do you want this door to be 30", 32" or 36" wide?

16. Driveways. Straight, curved, or turn around? You need to specify size (single car, double car, or larger), material (stone, blacktop, pavers, or concrete), and if it is heated or standard.

17. Patio, deck, or sunroom. Covered or open? What size? What material for the deck (wood deck, low maintenance deck, vinyl deck)? What material for the patio (stone, stamped concrete, standard concrete, patio blocks)? How many seasons for the sunroom (four season or seasonal)?

18. Landscaping (elaborate, basic, or none).

19. Grass (artificial, sod, or seed).

20. Optional items, which include security system, central vacuum, surround sound system, finished basement, outdoor watering system, or yard fencing.

CHAPTER 10

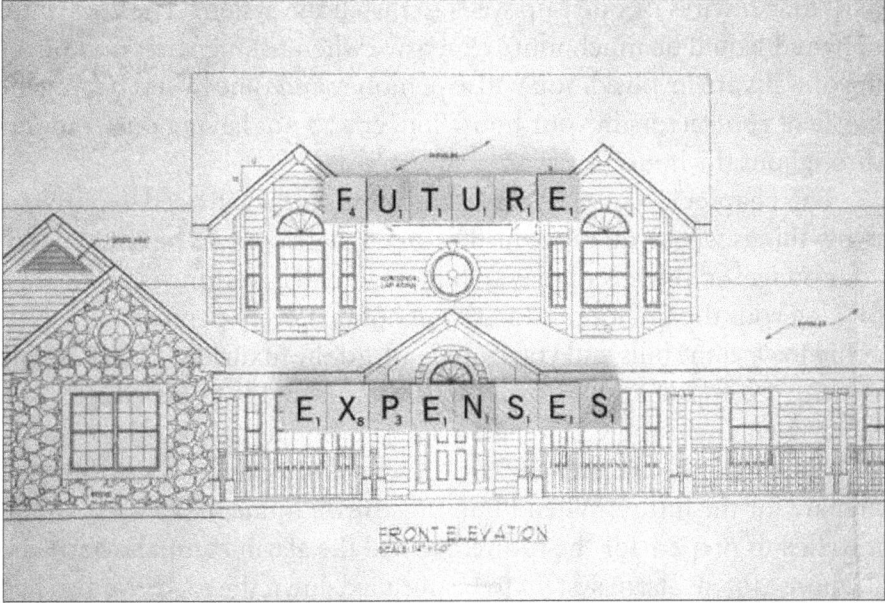

I included this topic because in the next several chapters, you are going to start building your dream home on paper. There are many things you would love to put into your house but cannot afford at this point. Between this chapter and the spreadsheet found in chapter 21, you are going to be able to keep track of all your dreams versus your wants. You are keeping track of these items so that after the house is done, you will continue to save money for years to come. During the building process, several items can be built into the structure to help save time and money in the future.

For example, a whole house sound system could cost four thousand to ten thousand dollars, depending on how elaborate the system is. Let us say that you would love to install this item in your dream home, but unfortunately, your budget does not allow this cost. But it is an item you really want in your house. One way around this is to have the house prewired for approximately a thousand dollars now, allowing you to save time and money when your budget does allow you to install it. If the house is prewired during the construction process, the installer will not have to fish wires or open up walls to install the system. The cost if not prewired would be much more expensive when fishing wires and opening of walls are involved. You will save money and time by not having the hassle of contractors in your house longer and not having dust and dirt throughout the house.

This chapter is also very important because you will need to purchase many things when you move in. These purchases should be entered into your budget so there is money to buy such items. Nothing is worse than owning your dream home and finding out that every penny you make is going toward the bills and you cannot afford the luxuries of life. Coming up with a comprehensive list of items you may want to install after you move in will help you get prepared for your budget

While your home is under construction, you can do a few things to prepare for the future. When I built my dream home, I had a few things installed to prepare for the future. We had the alarm company hardwire the house for an alarm system to be installed down the road. We also had a company prewire our house for sound. (Surround sound and a stereo system to play music throughout the home). We also had a future tube installed from the basement to the attic. The future tube allows us to feed the first floor from the basement and the second floor from the attic in the event that a future technology comes along. Below you will see a list of items that you may purchase within the first ten years of moving in.

1. Wallpaper
2. New inside furniture
3. New outdoor furniture
4. Throw rugs
5. Window treatments
6. Decorations for each room
7. Deck or patio
8. Seasonal or all season sunroom
9. Sunroom

10. Swimming pool
11. Children's play set
12. Fence for the yard
13. Landscaping
14. Lawn and garden tools
15. Lawnmower
16. Snow blower
17. Finishing the basement
18. Screen in your garage

CHAPTER 11

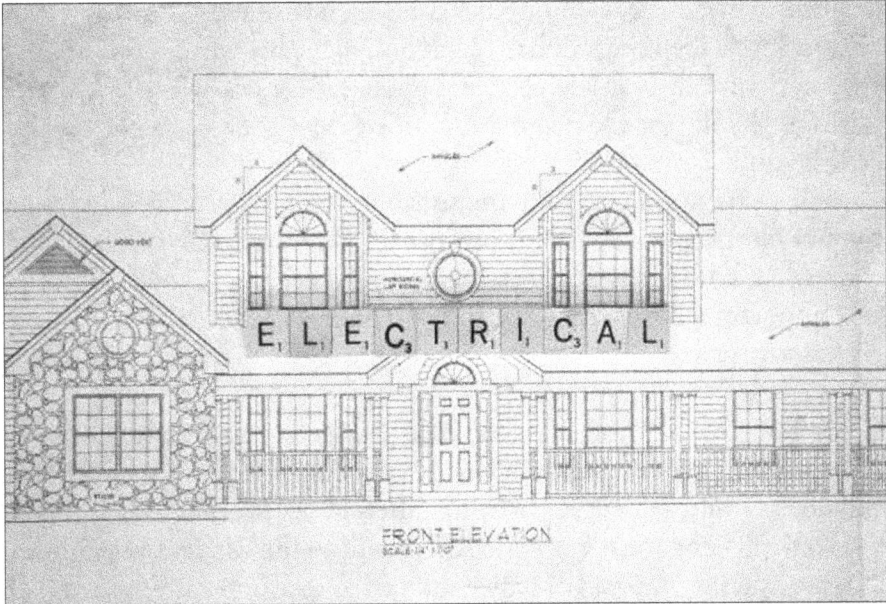

Builders will outsource the electrical to a licensed electrical subcontractor. The builder typically works with the same electricians on every home they build. Typically, builders only include the minimum electrical wiring necessary to keep your house in compliance with the codes. Local, state, and national codes have to be followed while wiring your house. Once you have narrowed the builder down to three to five builders, I recommend that you let each one know that they are in the final running. Let the selected builders know that you would like to meet with some of the subcontractors—in this case, the electrician. This meeting will allow you to find out what electrical items are included in the build. Refer to spreadsheet 2, found in chapter 21. Once you have found out what electrical items are included in the build, you will need to put together a list of any extra electrical items you want added to your build—a wish list. Refer to spreadsheet 3 in chapter 21. You will also be given a lighting allowance and a list of suppliers to pick out the lighting for your house. You need to know what this allowance is and compare it to your lighting spreadsheet to see if you need the builder to increase the allowance. Refer to spreadsheets 6 and 7 in chapter 21. These sheets will allow you to track both the lighting that the allowance will cover as well as what you may want to upgrade. Keeping good paperwork will allow you to stay on track during the negotiation process and prevents you from forgetting important items.

Whenever you meet with any subcontractor, you should always get contact information. Refer to spreadsheet 1 in chapter 21. This spreadsheet will help you stay organized in case you need to contact one of the subcontractors to answer any questions you have. If you like the subcontractor, you can use that company down the road for any extra work you may want to do to your house.

Below you will find a list of electrical enhancements that can be added to your home. As always, nobody knows what you like better than you do, so while you are researching different styles of homes, there will be electrical enhancements you want to add to the list. It is very important to always carry a pad of paper and pen to take notes about items you like or dislike so when it comes to putting your wish list together, items important to you are not overlooked.

1. **Main Electrical Control Panel:** This is where the power from your local power company connects to your house and distributes power throughout your house. The main breaker inside this panel is rated by amperage. Every electrical item connected through this box is rated in amps. It is important to have a large enough electrical panel to supply the power you require, both now and in the future. Every item in the house draws power, and this power is rated in amperage. The average main control panel in new residential construction is 150 amps or 200 amps. This number represents the amount of amperage your panel can draw at any one given time. There is no direct relationship between the main breaker and the cumulative total of breakers in the panel. For example, the total breakers in the panel can exceed the total size of the main breaker as long as the electrical engineer has deter-

mined that the total draw will not exceed the total amperage of the main breaker for any time. If this does happen, the main breaker will trip, preventing the wiring from overheating and causing a fire. The builder and electrician work together with the engineer/architect to design the electrical wiring of the house for typical residential usage. Before the building department will issue a certificate of occupancy, the entire electrical system needs to pass an inspection. I talk about this area because it is in your best interest to let the builder know what you intend to use in your house electrically so they can design this properly. For example: you run a catering business on the side and plan on using your house for cooking. To cook, you plan to install commercial ovens, mixers, and freezers. Depending on the power usage of these items, they may need to install a larger electrical panel than typically used in a residential house.

2. **Individual Circuit Breakers:** These breakers control each circuit in the house. Individual breakers range from 15 amps and up. The breaker size will depend on the usage of the circuit. Example: if there is a circuit feeding a bedroom with lighting and small items such as a TV and/or computer, a 15 amp breaker will be large enough for that circuit. If the circuit is running the kitchen, and you are going to have a dishwasher, refrigerator, and freezer, a 20 amp breaker would be needed. If you have a very large kitchen installed or you have a tendency to use many kitchen appliances at the same time, you may need to have several circuits put in the kitchen so breakers won't trip while you have a large entertaining project underway. The builders and engineers design houses and kitchens for typical usage, but if you like to entertain and need more kitchen outlets, this is the time to speak up and have your electric designed accordingly. When the electricians wire the house, they will use different sizes of wire for different sizes of breakers. This is why it is important for you to do your homework and make sure you know what each circuit might be used for, because after the fact it will be expensive to upgrade a circuit down the road. If you need to increase an area from 15 amps to 20 amps, it is not as simple as just changing the breaker. A 15 amp breaker only requires

14 gauge wires to run it safely, and a 20 amp breaker requires 12 gauge wires to run it safely. If you use a 20 amp breaker and run 14 gauge wires, the wire will overheat and cause a fire. So as you can see, the electrician cannot just change the breaker. They would also need to change the wiring. Below are examples of things you may want to consider.

    a. Kitchen: As I cited above, the kitchen can definitely be an area where breakers can trip. If you are the entertaining type and love to cook and put out big spreads, I suggest you make that known to the builder. Extra circuits should be installed in this area to prevent overloading circuits and tripping breakers during a very busy party.

    b. Garage: Will you use it for a refrigerator, freezer, compressor, or power tools? If the electricians install one 15 amp circuit in the garage and you use all the above items, you will most likely overload the circuit and keep tripping the breakers.

    c. Exterior: Will you be using electrical appliances, a hot tub, or holiday lights? You may want to consider installing a light switch for operating an outdoor outlet.

    d. Basement: Are you someone who has hobbies and uses power tools in the basement? You may want to have extra plugs installed in basement.

    e. Air conditioning: Are you installing central air, or do you just use a window unit at times? If you use a window unit, you should have a separate 20 amp outlet put under the window that will be used.

3. **House Lighting:** Selecting the right lighting may not be as easy as you think. Many new technologies are in the marketplace when it comes to residential lighting. Make sure you do your homework and do a lot of research during this stage. You are going to want to visit lighting stores, look at new homes, go to home shows, and research online.

The builder will give you a lighting allowance and a list of suppliers. Make certain that you can afford the lights you want. Below you will find a list of lighting ideas.

a. Recessed lighting
b. Ceiling fans
c. Dimmer switches
d. Track lighting
e. Closet lighting that comes on when door opens
f. Fluorescent lighting
g. Security spotlight on outside, near roof peaks
h. Lights built into staircases
i. Outdoor lighting mounted to brick work or siding

4. **Whole House Electric Generator:** Modern technology has progressed in this area. You can now get a generator that runs by itself. They use your natural gas or propane supplier. If the power kicks off, they automatically kick on and power most of your house. A battery is inside, and the generator periodically recharges the battery and tests the system. If you can afford it, this is definitely something you want to get. It does not have to be done while the house is under construction; it can be added easily enough after the house is complete.

CHAPTER 12

Most people do not think plumbing is an important item when building a new home as it can be an out of sight, out of mind item. Plumbing is very important infrastructure that every future homeowner should spend more time researching. When the house is designed and built, all state and local building codes are followed. But these only cover the basics of plumbing; modern construction has enhanced plumbing in a new home. This is why it is important for each future homeowner to spend quality time researching all options that new construction has to offer. As with all areas, please do yourself a favor and do your homework. It is worth any effort spent.

Plumbing in a new home construction includes but is not limited to all pumps, piping, faucets, valves, and any other item used to deliver potable water throughout the new home. It also covers any piping, drains, valves, pumps, or any other items needed to dispose of water borne waste. The term plumbing also refers to any water based heating systems, whether it be for heating the entire house, just an area of the home, or heated flooring. It also includes any gas piping required to supply any appliance, furnace, heaters, or fireplaces. This includes any fixtures, toilets, sinks, faucets, washer and dryer hookups, the dishwasher, and any exterior water supply.

To start with, you need to know where your house is going to be built. Are you going into a development with public water and sewer? Are you going to build in an area where you are going to need a septic system and well water? If you are going to build in an area where you will require well water or septic tanks, costs could get out of control in a hurry. Therefore, to keep your budget under control, you'll want to make sure you do your due diligence prior to making a final decision about where you are going to build.

If the land you looking to build on requires well water, you might want to check around with other homes in the area to see if there is a problem with well water. You can also check with local professional well drillers as they work in the local areas and can offer answers to these types of questions. Below is a list of questions you need to ask to help you make the right decision prior to buying land or signing a contract.

1. Is this an area where public water may be available in the future? In most cases, where they do run public water, you will be required to connect to it. Drilling a well that you are only going to use for one year is not going to be very cost effective. This cost can be prevented if you are willing to wait until the public water is run to the area.

2. How abundant is the water in the area? Do local homeowners have wells that dry up certain times of the year?

3. Is the well water in the area hard water? This could require you to add softeners, which is an additional expense.

4. Do local wells have sulfur water? If yes, what do local homeowners do to alleviate the sulfur water? This could also be an added expense, both up front and ongoing in the future.

5. How easy will it be to find water? Most professional well drillers are very good at what they do and can tell if water is on the land, how deep they will have to drill, and typically, how much water there will be when they get there. As I said before, this area could blow your budget out of control. It is incredibly important to find out up front. What if they have a hard time finding water? What if they need to drill deeper than originally thought? What if the water is bad? What if the water is low in supply? Will the solution to these issues result in passing their expenses to you, or do they guarantee to hit water? You should not leave these items to chance. You need to clearly work these out with the well driller or builder prior to signing the contract. Be sure the details with costs associated with them and the ones with no cost to the homeowner are documented as such within the contract.

If you are looking at land that requires a septic system, you are going to need to contact the local health department as well as a local septic system professional to find out what's involved and what the estimated cost will be for installing a septic system on that piece of land. If the property requires dirt, this cost could get out of control. Each county's health department has different requirements, so make certain you don't buy land or sign a contract until you know what the cost could be and what you are getting into.

As you found in chapter 11, you will also be given an allowance here. The allowance covers any fixtures you put in your house. You will need to set up a meeting to find out what items are covered under plumbing and how much your allowance is. In chapter 21, I developed two spreadsheets as an aid for your use. The first one, spreadsheet 4, allows you to track what you can purchase with the allowance you have been given by the builder. The second one, spreadsheet 5, allows you to create a wish list of items you would love to have in your house. You should prioritize this list. Once you have completed both spreadsheets, you will see if there is going to be an overage in the allowance for this area. You have to negotiate for more allowance, increase your budget enough to be able to include the high priority items, or settle for the basics.

Below you will find a list of plumbing ideas that you can add to your wish list, but as always, if you do your research by calling and visiting with plumbers, plumbing stores, and home shows, you should be able to add the items that will be most important to you.

1. **Exterior Water Faucets:** If you live in the Northern Hemisphere, you will want to make sure the plumber installs the proper outdoor hose faucets. Most building codes only require a shutoff valve inside the house to shut off water to outside hose faucet. This valve, when closed and drained, prevents the hose faucet from freezing and breaking open, causing a water leak. If you forget to close the valve and drain the faucet, this could be a very expensive repair. The plumber can install a faucet that automatically shuts off the water supply inside the freeze zone and drains it every time you shut off the valve. I highly recommend adding this to your wish list. These faucets are not very expensive and can save you a lot of headache down the road.

Exterior water supply with vent to prevent siphoning water back into public water supply form pools and to help drain faucet to prevent freezing

2. **Utility Sinks:** Another item I recommend is a utility sink in the garage; utility sinks are usually installed in conjunction with the laundry area. But a utility sink in the garage is always helpful for quick clean ups and for washing cars.

3. **Laundry Area:** If you are going to have the laundry area put on the first or second floor, it is very important to install a catch tray with drain under the washing machine. To my knowledge, this is not required by code as of yet. I did not have one installed and had a first floor laundry. The drum split on my brand new washing machine, and the water spilled onto the floor and kept running because the sensors in the machine did not tell the water to shut off the valve. Thankfully, I was home at the time and was able to minimize the damage. (The water did do some damage as the water spilled on the floor and down into the finished basement, all over our new pool table and carpet.) If I had left for the day, which I usually do, the water would have kept running, causing a lot of damage and inconvenience.

4. **Bathroom Sinks and Bases:** There are a host of different types and styles of sinks to choose from. There are deep bowl sinks, shallow bowl sinks, single sinks, and double sinks; however, they generally come in standard sizes that are typically designed in the house plans. I recommend you look at all the different styles and have this built into the initial cost. In addition to different sinks, there are different types of bases and base heights to choose from. You may require a lower height to accommodate a handicapped individual, or if you are simply taller than average, it may be uncomfortable for you to bend over a standard height sink while washing hands, brushing teeth, shaving, or putting on makeup.

5. **Hot Water Heaters:** You are going to want to research this in detail. Many different types are on the market, such as gas and electric with tanks that come in different sizes as well as gas and electric tankless hot water heaters, which also come in all different sizes. If you are going with gas, they offer power vented and draft style venting. One thing to consider is that if there is a major power outage in your area,

tankless, electric, and power vent hot water heaters require power. If the power goes out, you won't have any hot water. I have seen and utilized several different options; however, the design that I am the most impressed with is where the setup involves two fifty gallon, gas powered hot water heaters with natural venting installed. We have a large family, and during the morning hours, we tend to use a lot of hot water. At any given time, we may have two showers, a washing machine, and a dishwasher all in motion, yet we have never run out of hot water. Even during power outages, the hot water heaters have pilot lights that run on natural gas with natural venting. During a power outage, we might have to rely on candles, flashlights, and the fireplace, but we always have a hot shower.

Dual fifty-gallon hot water heaters to provide ample hot water for large families

6. **Water Softeners:** If you are going to have well water, this should be considered a "must have" item. If you have public water, it is more of a luxury. Many of these are on the market, and they can be installed relatively easily before or after the house is built. But this item should be added to your wish list.

7. **Sump Pump:** This is a required item for any new home with a basement, but most building codes only require sump pumps to be electric with a backup valve installed. I recommend looking into a backup pump in case of a power outage. Some pumps run with battery backup or run without power. This is an important item to research. In the event of a power outage, the last thing you need to deal with is having an area of your house flooded. FYI, some insurance companies will give you a discount on your homeowner's policy if you have a backup in place for the sump pump.

CHAPTER 13

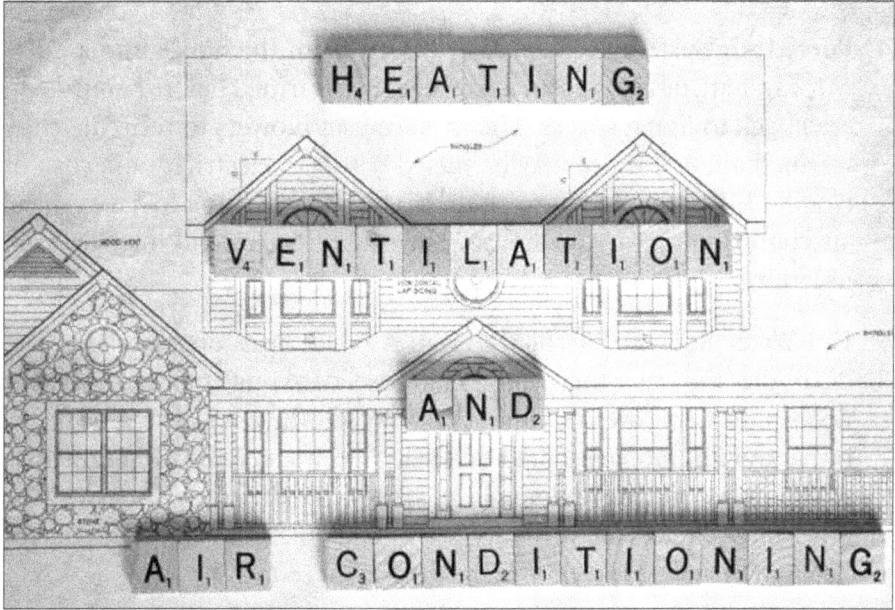

Several different types of heating, ventilation, and air conditioning (HVAC) systems can be installed in your house. Below I have listed a few heating systems. The engineer/architect will design a system that will work very nicely for the house being designed, and the builder typically has one or two trusted HVAC contractors. The builder and subcontractor will make sure the engineered system is installed properly, and the entire system will be inspected and passed as per state and local codes so there is not much for you to worry about. Below I have listed five different systems that can be used in a residential house, if you want to research them and see if there is a system that you would prefer, the engineer/architect can design the system of your choice. Numbers one and two are the most common and least expensive, numbers three through five are more expensive installs but can save you money in the long run.

There might also be some government assistance to help with the cost of numbers three through five. Your local and state websites can help you get started.

1. **Forced Air System:** A furnace draws air from the house into a duct-work system, taking it to an area where it is warmed before being delivered back to living spaces. The furnace uses blowers to recirculate the warmed air. A furnace may be fueled with gas, electricity, oil, coal, or wood. This system seems to be the best if you are going to have central air conditioning in your house. The same furnace and ductwork are used for both heat and air conditioning.

2. **Hot Water Radiant Baseboard Heat:** A boiler heats up water and then distributes the water through pipes to baseboard units mounted near the floor in the living area throughout the house. These boilers can be fueled by natural gas, propane, oil, or electricity. Electricity is the most expensive to run unless you are building in an area with reduced electric costs. The other three choices are very energy efficient, quiet, and able to keep temperature in living areas close to the thermostat setting.

3. **Geothermal Heating and Cooling System:** Fluid is pumped through pipes in the ground. The system draws heat cold from the ground and uses it in conjunction with your home heating and cooling system to help save energy.

4. **Solar heating systems:** This system harnesses the heat from the sun and transfers it to where you need it. Hot water, in conjunction with heat pumps for baseboard heating, it can be used to help heat pools and many more options. There are a lot of different systems out there. Most energy star companies can help you research and design a system that is right for you.

5. **Geosolar Heat System:** This is method uses both solar and geothermal systems to help double energy savings.

When picking a contractor, remember that sizing an HVAC system requires skill and experience. A poor design typically results in a system that doesn't deliver a consistent temperature from room to room and costs more to operate. But it can be even more serious than that. In very tight houses served by ductwork, poor design can lead to back drafting, a dangerous situation where flue gases are sucked back into the house, causing elevated levels of carbon monoxide, which is the silent killer.

The goal for a HVAC system is to provide proper airflow, heating, and cooling to each room. Top five things an HVAC system should have are listed below.

1. It should be properly sized to provide correct airflow and meet room by room calculated heating and cooling loads.

2. It should have sealed supply ductwork that will provide proper airflow.

3. It should be installed with a return system that is sized to provide correct return airflow.

4. It should have sealed return ductwork that will provide proper airflow to the fan and so air won't enter the HVAC system from polluted zones (e.g., fumes from autos and stored chemicals and attic particulates).

5. It should have proper burner operation and proper draft.

CHAPTER 14

Nothing is worse than having a brand new house and having your entertainment system look like a mess. Many companies out there do a very nice job helping you keep these items very neat and organized. Prewiring is the way to go.

Even if you cannot afford to purchase the entire system now, you should look into prewiring your house. Companies are out there that will prewire your house with prices starting at a couple hundred dollars and up. The cost is quite a bit less expensive and less messy than doing it after the house is built.

When you have your house engineered, the architect should be familiar with the type of home entertainment equipment that can be installed into your new home. Also, you should do your homework and research companies as well as other homeowners to see what is available for you. The local home show is a great way to actually put your hands on these items to play with them. Below is a small list of items that you can research to see if they match your needs.

1. **Whole House Sound:** This system will play music throughout your house. The main unit is located in one spot, and then you can have individual units with speakers installed in every other room in the house. These individual units allow you, via remote control, to adjust the sound and control the source of music you want to listen to.

2. **Security System:** This item absolutely should be prewired if not installed. Security companies will typically install the system with no upfront cost as long as you sign up for service with them. I found a company that prewired my house for no charge in hopes that it will lead to future service.

3. **Security Cameras:** These cameras not only record for security purpose but also can be used to monitor. These systems have come a long way over the years. The cameras can be accessed via computers or even smartphones so the homeowner can monitor the property at any time and from anywhere.

4. **Remote Lighting System:** You can also have the house wired so you can turn lights on and off from your computer, cell phone, or car.

5. **Phone Jacks:** With the day and age of cell phones, home phones are becoming less popular, but I recommend you still have enough phone jacks installed in your home. If you or a future homeowner ever opens a home based business, the jacks will come in handy for phones or fax. With that in mind, try to think of everywhere and anywhere you may need a phone or fax to make sure you have enough phone jacks installed.

6. **Cable Jacks:** Remember that as time goes on, the average homeowner changes the location of furniture in each room. Make sure you have enough jacks installed to accommodate these moves. The cost while the house is in the framed stage is far less than installing them after the house is finished and painted.

7. **Future Tube:** If you are building a two story house, I recommend that you have a future tube installed. This is a conduit that can be buried in the walls between the basement and the attic and allows wires to be fed through in case there is future technology that needs to be installed in each room through the house. This tube allows installers to access the second story through the attic and the first floor through the basement. Once again, this will save you money and a mess in the future.

8. **Prewire Fireplace:** If you are installing a fireplace, make sure you have this area prewired just incase you would like to install a flat screen TV above it. Make sure the architect designs this area with the proper heat protection for the wiring as well as proper fans to help protect your TV. As heat leaves the fireplace, it rises, so one would need to ensure that the TV wouldn't overheat.

CHAPTER 15

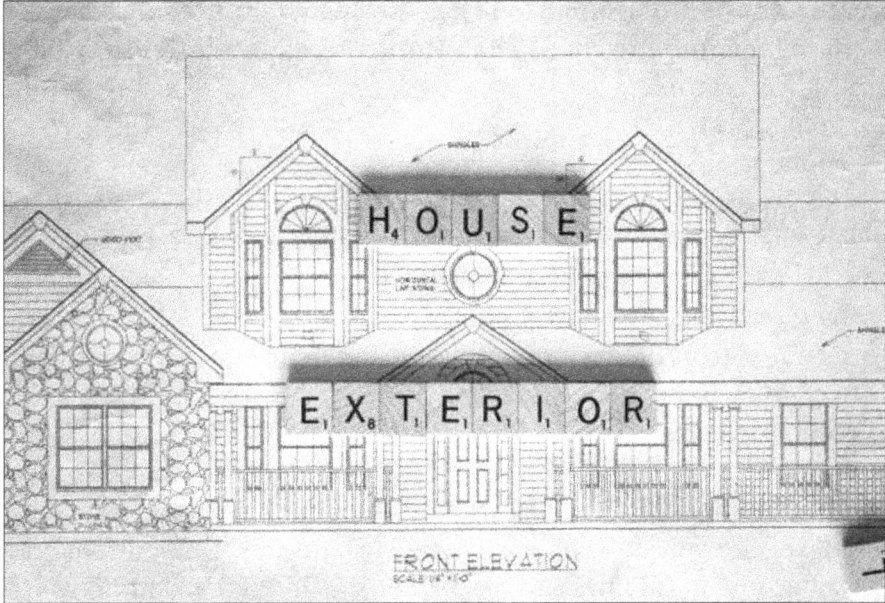

The exterior of your house is your first line of defense against the elements and insects. The weather can damage a house in areas that are not easily detected until the damage becomes extensive. Insects are a nuisance and can damage structural components of a building, creating extensive costs to the owner. Building codes cover these minimally, but the most effective way to protect your house from future damage is to have your architect design the house exterior with this thought in mind. This area might be the single most important part of saving money. The last thing you want to do is to spend money in the future for things that could have been prevented.

After the architect has designed the proper preventative measures, you need to make sure the builder understands these concepts and follows through with all subcontractors to make sure the items are installed correctly. You need to make sure you understand the multiple products that can be used for an exterior as well as the proper procedures of installation. You do not need to know how to install them; you just need to be up to speed on the proper techniques. Leave it to the professional to install. Below is a list of things that you need to look into to help defend your house against the elements and unwanted visitors.

1. **Foundation:** There are three types of conventional concrete foundations: poured concrete, concrete block, and post and pier. Size and acceptable types are regulated by building codes and are installed first. This is what is going to support the house. After these are installed, they need to be protected from the elements. The most common protection is to put some form of sealant on the surface. The second protection method is to make certain that no groundwater can damage it. Perforated pipe with pea size gravel is installed to direct ground water away from the foundation. The water most typically is directed to a sump pump, which then pumps the water away from the foundation. Make sure you do your own homework on this. Let your architect know of your findings and see if he or she thinks that your ideas will fit well in the house you are designing.

2. **Roof:** You should never cut costs on this area. It is exposed to more extreme weather, including sun, wind, rain, ice, and snow, than any other part of the house. After the house is framed, sheathing is installed on roof rafters, and the roofing is installed on top of that. Several different types of roofing can be used on a roof. There are asphalt and composition shingles, metal roofs, slate roofs, cedar roofs, and clay tile roofs. Roofing is a very expensive part of the house. A lot of money can be either saved or wasted here, which is why time should be spent to select the proper roofing type right for the climate. The architect needs to make certain that he or she designs the roof ventilation and that all bathroom fans are properly vented through the roof to the outside. Vents need to be exhausted through the roof and not just in the soffit. The attic needs to be the same temperature as the outside

so the roof does not overheat and become ruined. You also have to make sure that moisture does not build up in the attic space because too much moisture creates rot and mold, which are two things that will destroy the sheathing. It is, in my opinion, better to spend more money upfront and have a very expensive roof installed. Look for a longer warrantee and research the manufacturer to see how long they have been in business and how they have handles previous warrantee complaints. Also, find out from the builder who is installing the roof and make certain this subcontractor has a good reputation. Check them out online and through the local Better Business Bureau.

3. **Exterior Structural Sheathing (commonly known as plywood):** After the house is framed, sheeting is attached to the framing. This material is needed to tie in wall studs. It completes the strength of the framing and is a surface to which you attach your building finishes. Sheathing is made from different materials. Your architect will design the type of sheathing and thickness required by local building codes. If you are using a builder to supply working plans for your house, make sure you know what the specs call for before you sign. If you want a specific material, this is the time to negotiate change. Below is a list of the most popular type of sheathing.

   a. Plywood: This is a manufactured product made from thin layers of wood veneer. The layers of wood veneer are glued together, with each layer at 90 degree angles, thus providing better strength and more durability against cracking and shrinkage. The most common size is four feet by eight feet and half an inch thick. Plywood is a little more expensive than OSB but has more strength and resists water better if someday down the road you develop an undetected leak.

   b. OSB (Oriented Strand Board): This product is a manufactured wood product formed by layering strands of wood bonded with wax and resin adhesives. The material contains approximately 95 percent wood and 5 percent wax with resin adhesives. This product is less expensive but can vary in strength and durability. Your architect will design your house and recommend whether this product should be used.

c. Exterior Gypsum Board: Exterior gypsum sheathing is a water resistant product designed to attach to exterior sidewall framing as an underlayment for various exterior siding materials, such as wood, metal or vinyl siding, masonry veneer, stucco, shingles, etc. The panel is manufactured with a wax treated, water resistant core faced with water repellent paper on both face and back surfaces and long edges.

d. Exterior Nonstructural Sheathing: Commonly known as foam insulation board. This material has no structural integrity but does have insulating values.

4. **Building Façade:** This is commonly referred to as one side of the building—usually the front side. It is not uncommon to have the front side of the house finished with a different type of material (such as brick or stone). This is going to depend entirely on personal preference. The architect will be able to design this based on the homeowner's personal preference.

5. **Exterior Walls:** These walls can be covered with a variety of different materials. The final decision can vary between personal preference and regional weather factors. The architect and homeowner can decide the final material. Whatever material is used, just be certain the plans show the exterior sheathing is sealed before the installation of the exterior finish. This can be done with but is not limited to insulation board, building wrap, exterior tape, caulk, and construction felt paper. These building materials will help seal exterior walls to prevent the penetration by weather and any unwanted visitors.

6. **Windows:** There are many factors to consider when selecting windows. The minimum size is going to be mostly determined by

building codes in regards to egress laws, which pertain to escaping the building in case of emergency. All architects/engineers are very well versed in the rules and will design the house with this in mind. These regulations only pertain to the minimum size requirements. The maximum window size varies on what the homeowner prefers to have in the house. Prior to meeting with the architect or during the design of the house, time needs to be spent researching all the different windows that are available. There are several different types and styles of windows, so doing your homework is important.

7. **Doors:** In each home, there are front doors, side doors, back doors, doors from the garage to the living area, sliding doors, main garage doors, and overhead garage doors. How many of these appear depends on the type of home. Most homes are designed using the minimum requirements. I recommend looking at the different sizes available, starting with garage overhead doors. In some areas, most of the newer doors will be nine by seven, nine by eight, sixteen by seven, or sixteen by eight. However, there are many developments where the builder wanted a little different look from every other neighborhood and may have used ten foot or eighteen foot wide doors. On some older homes, fourteen foot and fifteen foot wide doors were used in some areas on a regular basis. Also, twenty to thirty years ago, eight foot wide, single car garage doors were very common, but as cars got bigger and trucks and SUVs became more popular, the standard door on many new homes was made wider and sometimes taller to accommodate larger vehicles. You need to consider what size vehicles you drive now and what size car you plan to drive in the future. In addition to the size, there is also style and color to consider. Front entrance doors come in different sizes, although the most common size is thirty six inches and comes in single or double doors. The most common doors are steel, wood, or fiberglass. Sliding doors are typically used to as an entrance to a deck or patio. They also come in different sizes.

8. **Gutters and Downspouts:** Gutters and downspouts make sure that all water and or melting snow from a roof is directed away from the exterior siding of the house and foundation. When the water hits the bottom of the downspout, make certain that the water is directed into a piping system that directs the water away from the foundation. This is extremely important, as the protection of the house exterior and foundation are critical for the longevity of the house itself.

CHAPTER 16

In the previous chapter, we discussed the first line of defense: the exterior of the house. In this chapter, I am going to discuss the second line of defense for energy savings through proper air sealing, insulation, and ventilation of the interior living space.

During the past decade, the home improvement industry has come a long way with making homes more energy efficient. This helps homeowners save on their heating and cooling bills and helps the environment. Some state and local building departments have kept up with it, and some have not advanced as much as others. The basic principle of making any building energy efficient is to create an envelope by completely encasing the building, preventing the inside and outside air exchange.

Here is an example of this. We all know that hot air rises, so in the winter, when we are heating our homes, the hot air will rise. If the attic space of the building is not properly insulated and the building is not properly air sealed, this will create a stack effect. The hot air will escape into the attic and out. As this happens, the escaping air needs to be replaced, so cold air from the outside gets sucked in through any crack it can (windows, doors, cracks in foundations, cracks between the wooden walls and the concrete foundation, holes where electrical wiring or cabling enters or exits the house, any piping between floors, and chimneys). This will make a building drafty, and your heating system will run more often, costing you more money. Right now is your opportunity to invest in your future. Building an energy efficient home will save you thousands of dollars over time and give you a comfortably warm home to live in. Below I have listed several ideas for making your house energy efficient, but in addition to these, you can do research on your own. There are many books, websites, and publications on this very topic.

Your first stop should be the US Environmental Protection Agency Energy Star website: www.enerystar.gov. This site is extremely helpful and will show you how you can build your new home and make it 30 percent more energy efficient than the typical new home build. Another area to visit is your state's Energy Star site. Most states offer incentives to help you build an energy efficient home. New York State is on the cutting edge with energy efficiency, so make certain you look at that site. The time you spend here is absolutely worth every minute. You need to discuss this with the engineer/architect and the builder. Let them know about your findings and what you would like to do.

1. **Air Sealing:** Prior to insulating the house, every crack and hole should be caulked, from the concrete to the roof. Building codes require fire caulk be used to fill in any hole between floors where wires go through. This procedure is to help prevent the spread of a fire between floors. But this procedure does in fact help with energy efficiency by eliminating the stack effect. If your local codes do not require this, make certain that the builder builds this into the price to make certain it is done. In addition to the holes where wires go through, make sure caulk or foam is added to gaps or cracks in the sill plate, piping, chimney, and cabling. Make certain all the windows and doors are properly

insulated or spray foamed prior to the final trim work installation. Then the trim should be properly caulked prior to painting.

2. **Insulation:** There are many insulation companies out there. Some are very good and some are very bad. As with any skilled trade, the faster they get the job done, the more money the company makes. This is not your concern; your concern is to make certain the job is done correctly so that you can save money over time. Make sure you express your concerns with the builder from day one to make certain no corners are cut here.

   a. Wall Insulation: Insulation starts at the sill plate and ends at the attic space. Between each wall stud, there is an opening, these openings are insulated from top to bottom; the insulation needs to be properly attached to the top of the studs so that the insulation does not sag inside the wall pocket, creating an open pocket at the top of the wall. (Remember, hot air rises. So if the insulation sags and there is an open pocket at the top of the wall, this is where your heat will escape.) I have heard some contractors tell the customer that the wallboard will hold it in place, Yes, it will stop insulation from falling into the room, but the wallboard is not going to stop it from sagging inside the wall cavity.

   b. Attic: The ceiling and attic area have a very important part in keeping energy costs down as well as keeping your house warm and draft free. For starters, it is a bad idea to use the attic area for storage. I know that, over the years, many people have used it for that purpose, but let me explain why this is a bad idea. The attic area should always be kept as close to the outside temperature as possible to protect your roof. If the attic area gets too hot in the summer, your roof will get too hot, and the shingles will be damaged. If the attic gets to warm in the winter, snow can melt prematurely and cause ice dams. Ice dams damage roofing by allowing water under the roof and freezing, causing the roof to peel upward. This will create damage to the roofing and gutters and ultimately creates leaks, which in turn damages roof sheathing, roof rafters, insulation, ceilings, and walls. So, with that being said, you can see why it is critical that this area of the house get the proper attention it needs. A few things need to be done for the attic to remain as close to outside temperature as possible. The first thing is making sure that there are enough soffit and roof vents to allow proper flow of air so the attic does not overheat or trap moisture. The soffit vents are located at the bottom of roof, right near the gutters. The vents are facedown and are perforated or screened so that unwanted visitors are not able to enter. The second thing is making certain there are proper baffles installed to allow the air to cycle from soffit to roof vent. Inside the attic area, baffles allow the insulation to not block the flow of air. On or near the top of the roof, roof vents are installed. Either they install a ridge vent, which runs the entire length of the peak, or square vents are installed along the back side of the roof. In my opinion, the ridge vent is less likely to leak when installed properly and offers a more consistent flow of air from the soffits. The engineer will design the proper amount of vents and baffles, and the builder, along with the inspector, will inspect to make sure that they are installed properly. I recommend that you stay on top of the builder to make certain this task is performed correctly. And the last thing is to make sure that there is enough insulation installed.

3. **Ceiling Insulation:** Building designs, unless otherwise directed, will use the building codes as the minimum standard. This includes insulation. The minimum insulation level, in my opinion, is simply not enough. I would speak to the builder and have more insulation added. The money spent on extra insulation will pay for itself in a short time and start saving you money.

4. **Ventilation:** The ventilation in a house is very important to prevent moisture buildup, which can cause mold, mildew, and rot. All bathroom fans need to vent to the outside. Typically, they are vented to the soffit, although they can be vented through the roof. Either way,

make sure that they don't just drop the vent pipe in the soffit. Make sure they use an actual soffit vent that gets hard piped into the soffit. If they install a roof vent, make sure they install it before installing the roof to allow the area to be properly sealed. In either case, make certain that they hard pipe all vents. In addition to the bathrooms, your cloths dryer also needs to be vented to the outside. If the dryer is gas, they need to use hard piping. If it is electric, they can use flexible piping. Whether you have gas or electric, make sure they hard pipe all the way to the dryer. I also recommend that you have a vent installed in the kitchen that is also hard piped to the outside. This helps vent unwanted cooking odors as well as any extra moisture from cooking.

5. **Smoke and Carbon Monoxide Detectors:** Most building codes require hardwired smoke detectors be installed when building a new home, but the building codes do not require hardwired carbon monoxide detectors. I highly recommend that you install a hardwired carbon monoxide detector and a hardwired smoke detector on each level of the house. Have the builder include these in the quote. In addition to this, I also recommend that you have battery operated detectors installed on each floor as well. Safety should never be taken lightly; this house is going to be home for your family, friends, pets, and you. If there is a problem with a defective appliance or a fire, every second counts to get everyone out of the house. This is why having more is always a great choice. Keep in mind that if you have a power outage, the hardwired detectors will not work, and this is probably the time you need them the most. During power outages, homeowners use things like candles for light and portable generators for power, both of which create a fire and carbon monoxide hazard. The lives of you and your loved ones depend on this, so spend the extra few bucks and get it done.

CHAPTER 17

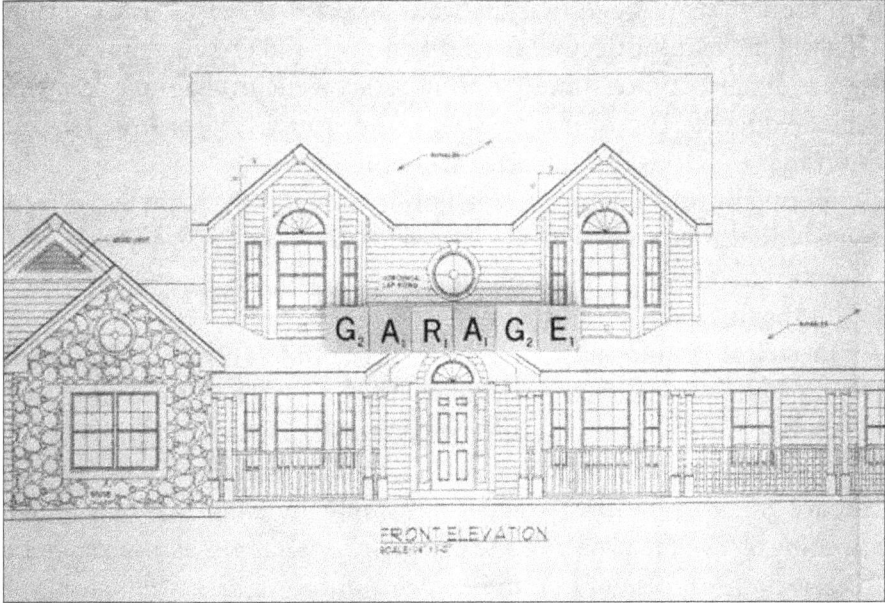

Your garage is not a critical part of the build, but as any homeowner can attest, it is a critical part of your life. From my experience, a garage can never be too big. Before you sign with the builder, you will need to decide what size garage you would like. The difference in price between a two car and three car garage when designing your home is less money than you would expect. Typically, builders invest the minimum amount of time and money in the garage; they bring it up to code and stop there. Every state and town varies slightly on codes. This would not be of too much concern for you, as the building inspector would require the garage to meet code prior to releasing any certificate of occupancy. What is a concern for you is finishing off the garage for your personal use.

Most builders finish the garage as basically as possible. This would include but is not limited to fireproof drywall on all the walls and double fireboard on any wall adjacent to a living space. All drywall seams require one coat of joint compound, but it is not sanded or painted. You will have one electrical outlet on each wall and one on the ceiling for a garage door opener.

I highly recommend that the walls be painted before you move in. This will prevent the drywall from discoloring and growing mold. If you are handy and do not mind painting, I recommend that you paint the garage yourself. The money you will save would be worth it. Keep in mind that the drywall contractor will only be putting one coat of joint compound on and will not sand it. For the garage, this might be OK with you. If you want the garage walls to look perfect, like the inside walls, you may want to have the builder include the price for the drywall contractor to put the final coat on and sand it.

Electrical in the garage is usually basic, and as I talked about earlier, the basic wiring includes ceiling lights, an outlet on the ceiling for a garage door opener, and an outlet on each wall. Usually, the garage is tied into a breaker from a different part of the house. Depending on what you are going to use the garage for, this may be enough power. If you are going to use the power in the garage for such items as a refrigerator, freezer, power tools, air compressor, or outdoor Christmas lights, you may want to consider having a dedicated 20 amp breaker installed for just the garage.

You also want to make sure the wiring for the garage door opener is installed in the garage, and if you are going to have a central vacuum installed in the house, make sure that they put a connection in the garage because it is great for vacuuming your cars out.

Another important detail is sealing the concrete floor. Sealing the concrete floor is important for two reasons: one, to eliminate dust carried into the house, and two, it promotes easier cleanup of the floor without leaving stains (oil, gas, paint, stain, grass, and dirt). Another great idea is to have a utility sink installed in the garage. Utility sinks in the garage are quite handy, especially when it comes to performing exterior maintenance and their associated cleanups. It's a bonus when washing your vehicles.

CHAPTER 18

Driveways can be made out of many different types of materials, such as asphalt, concrete, paving blocks, and a few other products. Driveways can also be made in different sizes and shapes. The type of product used has to do with where the home is being built, the weather, and price. The size and shape will depend on both the pricing and size of the lot. The engineer/architect will help you walk through the different options you have to choose from. Make sure you research all other homes in your area so you get an idea of what is built in the area you are building. Another way is to reach out to contractors that specialize in driveways. There are concrete contractors, asphalt paving contractors, and landscaping companies that use concrete pavers. Once you have researched different ideas, run your ideas past the engineer/architect to figure out which one fits your needs and price point.

There are also some outside the box ideas that could be used. My favorite is the heated driveway. This is awesome in areas where snow is prevalent. Piping is placed below the concrete driveway and hot water is pumped through the piping. This hot water heats the driveway above the freezing mark, so the driveway is always clear from snow and ice. Keep in mind that this type of system costs money every month during the winter months, as a boiler heats the water and uses fuel to run.

CHAPTER 19

THE FINAL INSPECTION

FRONT ELEVATION
SCALE 1/4" = 1'-0"

Just before the closing date, the builder will schedule a final walk through with the future owner of the home. This is in addition to the building department's final inspection. All buildings require a CO (certificate of occupancy) before anyone can occupy the property. The local building department performs the final inspection and will issue the proper paperwork so the building can be sold and occupied. This inspection makes certain that the building is safe for occupancy and that all building codes are met.

The final inspection you are going to perform is to make certain that there are no imperfections in workmanship and that all products and colors are up to your requirements. During this walk through, you need to make certain everything you are paying for, including items from the change orders, were delivered. Open and close doors and windows and be sure appliances, lights, fans, and garage door openers are all functional. Check the paint job to ensure there are no rough areas and no holes or gaps, including all trim work. Look at the hardware installed on the front of cupboard doors to ensure they are installed correctly.

The best practice is to take your time, engage a couple friends or family members, and go through the entire house, top to bottom, interior and exterior. Any issues found will need to be documented, prioritized, and tracked onto a spreadsheet (called the Issues Log) until they are resolved. You can create a spreadsheet of your own or use the one I created in chapter 21. Most builders refer to an Issues Log as a "punch list." Called by either name, they perform the same function.

Most builders are reasonable with completing follow up repairs, but a few out there are not as reliable. This final inspection is your last opportunity to ensure that anything and everything you were expecting as part of your build has been completed and functional. Anything that is not should be on your Issues Log. You will give a copy of it to the builder and your attorney once the final inspection has been completed.

CHAPTER 20

The final closing, just like the sale or purchase of any house, is the last step of the process when the transfer of ownership occurs between the builder and the new homeowners and full payment is remitted to the builder. Once you leave the closing table, there are no opportunities for further negotiations. You will, more than likely, need to hire a real estate attorney to manage the closing of your new build. That being said, I cannot stress enough the importance of retaining an attorney whose focus is real estate law, especially new builds. The practice of law is very complex and vast; to expect any attorney to be able to master and represent all areas of the law is almost impossible. Therefore, choosing the proper attorney for the proper job is going to ensure that you will be getting the best results from the money paid.

Keep in mind that your attorney is an attorney, not a builder or contractor, so he or she will get you through all the legalities and paperwork and will probably have great suggestions and recommendations to share with you.

It is in your best interest to hold off on closing until your issues have been resolved. However, in some situations, time is more of a factor and the need to close demands adherence to a schedule. If that should be the case, be sure to have a copy of your punch list updated to reflect any open issues that still exist to review at the closing table. You need to get the builder to sign off on the changes. The builder is responsible for resolving the issues after closing, so be sure to have a reasonable time-frame associated with the items. Don't let the builder off the hook for completion of these tasks and don't assume responsibility to complete them on your own and at your expense.

Let me give you an example. The builder is responsible for taking care of your lawn, including its grading and seeding, etc. However, if the weather did not permit the builder to complete this task before closing, you need to protect yourself at the closing table. How? By having this task added to the punch list and holding the builder accountable for completing it when weather permits. If the builder wants to close, the builder should make the necessary efforts to resolve any outstanding issues.

Another way to protect yourself at the closing table when outstanding issues need to be resolved or when incomplete work exists is to have a portion of the closing funds, which would normally be paid to the builder at the closing table, be put into an escrow account. This is not an unusual practice. Just prior to closing, review your punch list with your attorney to see if he or she recommends placing enough of the closing funds into an escrow account to cover the aggregate expenses of completing all remaining open items on your punch list in the event that you need to complete them on your own. This way, there's incentive for the builder to finish your list, but be sure that everything on the list is completed to your satisfaction before having your attorney release the funds from the escrow account to the builder.

CHAPTER 21

Tools to keep you in control

In this chapter, I have displayed several examples of spreadsheets to allow all future homeowners the tools to save money and stay in control. By purchasing this book, you have already taken the first step toward a successful build. Getting familiar with this chapter and making it a part of the build process will be the second step toward success. I had these sample spreadsheets printed in this book to show you what they look like. I have also made available to you these sheets and many others to download and use on my web site. These spreadsheets are free for owners of this book. Just visit my website, www.controlyourbuild.com. Click on the "TOOLS" tab and type in the user ID and password.

User id: controlyourbuild
Password: tools

After you have downloaded and printed the spreadsheets, make sure you put them into a three ring binder and start doing your home-work. Fill in each spreadsheet with as much information as you can. After this entire workbook is filled out, it will give you the opportunity to sit back and make an educated decision.

1. **Contact Information:** This form should be used to mark down every contractor who will perform any work. Keep this information in a safe place. This information will come in handy throughout the build process and will come in handy after you have closed on the house. The builder is ultimately responsible for all warrantees on the house, but if some unknown circumstance arises where the builder is not able to help with a future problem, this contact sheet will then become your best friend. In addition to warrantee items, these contractors are familiar with the home and might be able to save you money on future projects you may have.

	Contractor Information
NAME:	
ADDRESS:	
CITY/STATE/ZIP:	
CONTACT PERSON:	
OFFICE PHONE #:	
CELL #:	
	Contractor Information
NAME:	
ADDRESS:	
CITY/STATE/ZIP:	
CONTACT PERSON:	
OFFICE PHONE #:	
CELL #:	
	Contractor Information
NAME:	
ADDRESS:	
CITY/STATE/ZIP:	
CONTACT PERSON:	
OFFICE PHONE #:	
CELL #:	

2. **Electrical Items Included in price:** This spreadsheet allows you to see what electric items are covered under the basic build. As I discussed in chapter 11, you can add many options, so make sure you document all items the builder covers. Use the next sheet to add any items you want to add to your wish list.

Electric Items Included in price

	TASK DESCRIPTION	Quantity/Size	Manufacturer
1	Main Electric Service Size?		
2	Outside Lighting (how many? Including Security lighting?)		
3	Outside Power Outlets (how many? What size Breaker? Switched inside for holiday lighting?)		
4	Garage (Lighting? Garage door opener?)		
5	Garage Outlets (do you need additional power for tools)		
6	Basement Lighting		
7	Basement Outlets (are you going to finish the basement in the future?)		
8	Kitchen Power (how many circuits? What size Breaker)		
9	Bathroom Electric (TV hook up for Master Bath?)		
10	Bathroom Vent Fans (What Quality?)		
11	Electric outlets per room?		
12	Cable outlets per room?		
13	Phone Jacks per Room?		
14	Security system?		
15	Family Room (Surround Sound System? Wall Mounted TV?)		

3. **Electrical Extras Wish List:** This spreadsheet allows you to keep track of extra electrical items you may want to add to your house. In chapter 11, I gave you a great starting point to help put this list together. Keep in mind that this is a wish list, not a list of requirements. However, I do recommend that you prioritize the list so when it does come down to having extra money in the budget, you are able to better decide where the money is best spent. After you enter all the electrical extras, get an estimate for how much the cost will be and enter this number to the spreadsheet. Keeping track of these items will help you keep your budget under control. When it comes down to negotiating with the builder, you may just get some of these items thrown in if the builder is hungry for the work.

Contractor Information

NAME: _____

PHONE NUMBER: _____

Electrical Extras Wish List

	Description of Extra	Quantity/Size	Cost
1			
2			
3			
4			
5			
6			
7			
8			
9			
10			
11			
12			

4. **Plumbing Included in the Build:** This spreadsheet allows you to see what plumbing items are covered under the basic build. As I discussed in chapter 11, you can add many options, so make sure you document all items the builder covers. Use the next sheet to add any items you want to add to your wish list. The builder usually has a particular type of plumbing fixture for each house that is built, although you are given an allowance to pick out what you want. The difference in the cost is your responsibility to pay. Use this spreadsheet to keep track of the plumbing fixture costs as well as the style of fixtures that the builder has included into the cost of the build. All builders have a list of suppliers they use throughout each build process. Find out who the suppliers are and visit. While you are at each supplier, you should research two things. The first item would be finding out what type of fixtures you can purchase with the allowance set for your build. The second item would be to find fixtures that you would love to have in your dream house. When it comes down to negotiating with the builder, you may just get some of these items thrown in if the builder is hungry for the work.

Contractor Information

NAME: _____

PHONE NUMBER: _____

Plumbing Items Included in Price

	TASK DESCRIPTION	Quantity/Size	Manufacturer
1	Water Pump		
2	Water Heaters (one or two gas or electrical what size)		
3	Type of Toilet (standard or custom)		
4	Exterior Spigots (how many location)		
5	Utility tub (Basement 1st floor or Garage)		
6	Laundry Hook ups (Basement, first floor, second floor is water catch pan included)		
7	Type of water faucets for all sinks, tubs and showers		
8	Tubs and showers units (sauna tub, accessible tub, tile tub, on piece tub)		
9	Gas piping (outdoor heaters or grills indoor range tops, stoves or fireplaces)		

5. **Plumbing Extras Wish List:** After you have researched the plumbing allowances, use this spreadsheet to enter any extras or items that you wish to have installed into your dream home. Keep in mind that you do not have to just shop where the builder recommends. You can shop online at an auction or at any other supply store you choose. Just keep in mind that if you do purchase something from somewhere outside of the builder's list, the builder will not be responsible for the warrantee or delivery of items. Make certain that if you go this route, the savings outweigh the extra work on your side. I have found that if you are doing your homework, the savings can be significant.

Contractor Information

NAME: _____

PHONE NUMBER: _____

Plumbing Extras Wish List

	Description of Extra	Quantity/Size	Cost
1			
2			
3			
4			
5			
6			
7			
8			
9			
10			
11			
12			

6. **Lighting Included in Price:** This spreadsheet will allow you to itemize each light and help you track this expense. You may find that you need to increase the allowance or take money leftover here to add somewhere else in the project. When building a house, the builder will give you an allowance and a list of suppliers to pick your lighting fixtures for the house. Most allowances allow for basic lighting fixtures, so make sure you do a good job selecting lighting. Some lights can get very expensive. With that being said, go out and have a lot of fun, but just be careful.

Contractor Information

NAME: _____

PHONE NUMBER: _____

Lighting Included in Price

	Light and Location	Quantity/Size	Manufacturer
1			
2			
3			
4			
5			
6			
7			
8			
9			
10			
11			
12			
13			
14			

7. **Lighting Extras Wish List:** This spreadsheet allows you to keep track of any special lighting you may want to add to your house. Many different ideas are out there as far as lighting goes, and the sky is the limit. There is everything from basic to very elegant and extremely expensive lighting. As you are doing your homework, you will discover that lighting does have a factor in what type of feel your house has. You can go with fancy chandeliers or simple recessed lighting. One thing to keep in mind is that if you choose to go with recessed lighting, they become more difficult to change down the road. If you decide to go with the traditional lighting fixtures of chandeliers, they can be upgraded fairly easily down the road. Keeping track of these items will help keep your budget under control. When it comes down to negotiating with the builder, you may just get some of these items thrown in if the builder is hungry for the work.

Contractor Information

NAME: _____

PHONE NUMBER: _____

Lighting Extras Wish List

	Description and Location	Quantity/Size	Cost
1			
2			
3			
4			
5			
6			
7			
8			
9			
10			
11			
12			

8. **Appliance List:** The builder will give you an allowance and a list of suppliers. The builder prefers that you go to specified suppliers for a couple of different reasons. The first reason is that they are trusted, and the builder has a good working relationship with them. The second reason is that the more customers the builders send to the supplier, the less expensive the pricing gets. Do not let this be the determining factor for where you want to buy. The determining factor for you should be getting the most for your money. Using the next two spreadsheets, mark down your appliances and your allowances so you can make the correct decisions when you buy. I recommend watching out for sales and purchasing your appliances with your money and having that receipt deducted from the closing table. Either you can lower the mortgage amount or you can get a check refunded to you from the closing. Either way, this is an area that you can save a lot of money or upgrade to better appliances. But before you start purchasing any appliances, make certain you have the correct size and location for that appliance. Once you have that information, start looking for businesses going out of business, auctions, or just sales at retail locations. Keep in mind that you may be responsible for delivery and installation of any appliance that you pick out. Check with your builder on this to make sure you are aware of the situation. Also, keep in mind that if you purchase the appliance early in the build process, you may need to find a place to store it until the builder is ready for it.

Supplier Information

NAME: _____

PHONE NUMBER: _____

Appliance List

Appliance	
Manufacturer	
Model #	
Color	
Price	
Allowance	
Price Difference	

Supplier Information

NAME: _____

PHONE NUMBER: _____

Appliance List

Appliance	
Manufacturer	
Model #	
Color	
Price	
Allowance	
Price Difference	

9. **Change Order Estimate:** This spreadsheet should be used whenever there is a change to the original contract or engineered plans. Make certain it is filled out completely and signed by all parties. Do not leave things to chance—protect yourself.

Contractor Information

DATE: _____

NAME: _____

ADDRESS: _____

CITY/STATE/ZIP: _____

CONTACT INFORMATION: _____

Change order Estimate

TASK DESCRIPTION	MATERIAL	LABOR
Sub Total		

Authorization

ESTIMATED START: _____

DATE: _____

CUSTOMER: _____

CUSTOMER: _____

CONTRACTOR: _____

DATE: _____

10. **Flooring Included in price:** The builder usually has a particular type of flooring designed for each room of the house. It could be carpet, tile, hardwood, or some other type of flooring. Use this spreadsheet to keep track of the flooring cost as well as the types of flooring that the builder has included into the cost of the build. All builders have a list of suppliers that they use throughout each build process. Find out who the suppliers are and visit them. While you are at each supplier, you should research two things. The first item would be finding out what type of floor you can purchase with the allowance set for your build. The second item would be to find flooring you would love to have in your dream house. Write that information on the next spreadsheet. Once you have written all items down, they become real and easier to track.

Contractor Information

NAME: _____

PHONE NUMBER: _____

Flooring Included in Price

	Type and Room	Quantity/Size	Manufacturer
1			
2			
3			
4			
5			
6			
7			
8			
9			
10			
11			
12			

11. **Flooring Extras Wish List:** The builder will give you an allowance and a list of suppliers to visit to select the flooring. You can choose any style or quality of flooring, but keep in mind that they only w a certain amount budgeted for this expense. During your negotiation with the builder, if you already know that you need more money here, it can be added. Depending on how hungry the builder is for work, you may be able to get some type of upgrade thrown in.

Contractor Information

NAME: _____

PHONE NUMBER: _____

Flooring Extras Wish List

	Type and Room	Quantity/Size	Cost
1			
2			
3			
4			
5			
6			
7			
8			
9			
10			
11			
12			

12. **Future Items to Purchase/Install after Build:** You want to use this spreadsheet for two reasons. One reason is to make sure you have enough money after you move in, and the second reason is that if there are any items you want to install but can't afford, now this is the time to preinstall items that will help offset cost and save time down the road. To start with, there are items like window treatments; wall decorations; throw rugs; animal rugs; shelving in basement; shelving in the garage; extra furniture for areas like a spare bedroom or basement; and beds, dressers, basement furniture, and outdoor patio furniture. In addition to those items, you also need to purchase items to help maintain your property, like a lawn mower, snowblower, weed trimmers, shop vacuum, rakes, shovels, brooms, and miscellaneous hand tools. I understand that most people already own these items, but you need to keep them in mind just in case you need to replace worn or broken items. After you have moved into your dream home, homeowners typically will install certain items within the first five years. They include but are not limited to a deck or patio, awnings or sunrooms, a pool or hot tub, and a recreation room in the basement. Use this spreadsheet to write down any future items that might spend money on after you move into your dream house. Nothing is worse than moving into your dream home and finding out that you can't afford it or tearing out new walls or siding to install something that could have been done during the build, allowing you to save time and money.

Future Items to Purchase/Install after Build

	ITEM	Supplier/Contractor	Estimated Cost
1			
2			
3			
4			
5			
6			
7			
8			
9			
10			

Sub Total _____ $

Labor Cost

TOTAL EXPENSE _____

13. **Project Timeline:** Every builder does things just a little differently, so this timeline could vary from builder to builder. For the most part, all builds will travel in this order. Keep in mind that the builder wants to be paid for the job, so the project will be kept on track. The builder is not paid until the closing, so builders will keep things moving along. This sheet is primarily designed to help the future homeowner. It allows future homeowners to keep up with their end. There are going to be items that you are responsible for, such as selecting colors, cabinets, flooring, roofing, brick, siding, and many more. The last thing you want is to do while you are building the home of your dreams is to forget about an item and then have to make your mind up in a short time, thus increasing the possibility of choosing a product, color, or style that you are not going to be happy with. This sheet will also help you during the planning stage, as it will stimulate your thinking on many items.

Project Timeline

	Description of Task	Started	Completed
1	Building Permits		
2	Excavation Work		
3	Concrete Footings		
4	Foundation Walls		
5	Waterproofing Concrete Walls		
6	Foundation Inspection		
7	House Framing		
8	Rough Framing Inspection		
9	Roofing Installed		
10	Exterior Windows Installed		
11	Exterior Doors Installed		
12	Electrical Roughing		
13	Plumbing Roughing		
14	HVAC Roughing		
15	Fireplace Roughing		
16	Optional Items Roughing		
17	Mechanical Roughing Inspection		
18	Insulation Installation		
19	Insulation Inspection		
20	Interior Wall Finish (Drywall)		
21	Painting		
22	Interior Trim Work		
23	Cabinetry Installation		

24	Countertop installation		
25	Tile Work		
26	Mechanical Finish		
27	Interior Flooring		
28	Sidewalk Installations		
29	Driveway Installations		
30	Patio Installations		
31	Final Landscaping		
32	Final Interior Installations		
33	Final Drywall Touch Ups		
34	Final Painting Touch Ups		
35	Final Cleanup		
36	Final Inspection		
37	Final Walk Through		

14. Final inspection:

Final Inspection

Date	Description	Issue Owner	Priority H/M/L	Closed Y/N	Date Closed	Post-Close?	Exp Date of Resolution	Comments

CHAPTER 22

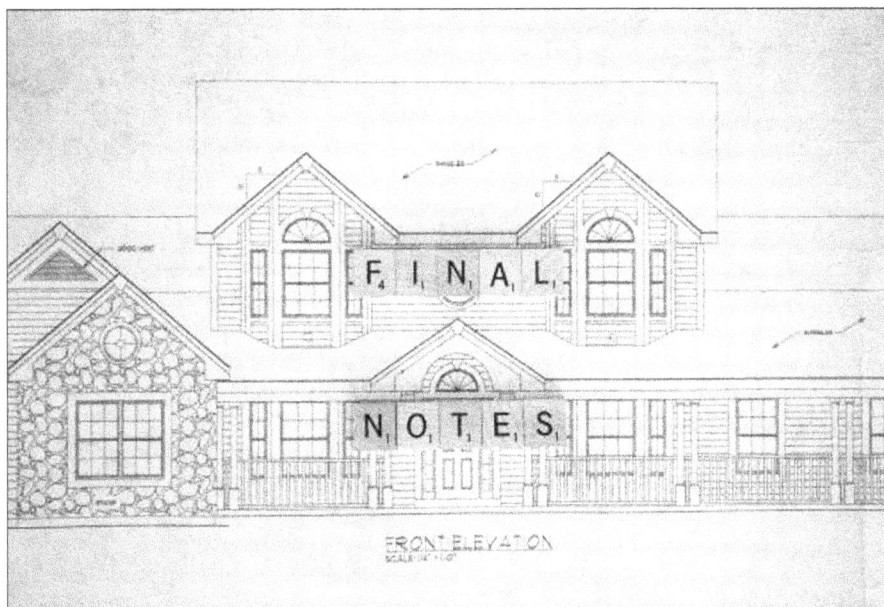

I have covered a lot of information in this book. As you can see, you need to do a tremendous amount of homework if you want your dream home to become a reality. I firmly believe that if you truly want something, you need to go out and get it! That something is not going to just come to you. You need to invest the proper amount of time, effort, and resources required to accomplish your goals. Reading this book just once is not enough to get the job done. You need to have this book become a part of you. The more time you spend researching the answers to your questions, the more likely your dream home will turn out to be truly a dream home.